To Art —

Merry Christmas 1983 —

a Happy, Funny New
Year to you — and
here's a good start —

Bev

From Approximately

Coast to Coast . . . It's

THE BOB AND RAY SHOW

From Approximately Coast to Coast ... It's THE BOB AND RAY SHOW

BOB   **A**   RAY
N
ELLIOTT   **D**   GOULDING

Foreword by Andrew A. Rooney

NEW YORK

Atheneum

1983

All photographs courtesy of Bob Elliott. Photograph on p. xvi by Ann Brodsky. Photograph on p. 128 from Frederic Lewis/French.

Library of Congress Cataloging in Publication Data

Elliott, Bob.
    From approximately coast to coast . . . It's the
Bob and Ray Show.

    I. Goulding, Ray.   II. Title.
PN1991.77.B6E44   1983   791.44′72   83-45069
ISBN 0-689-11395-1

TO

Tom Koch

FOR HELP BEYOND MEASURE

Foreword

BY ANDREW A. ROONEY

Bob and Ray have three distinct personalities. There's Bob's, there's Ray's and there's Bob and Ray's. Both Bob and Ray are interesting to meet separately because two duller people you never talked to. Every Sunday morning I meet funnier people down at the news store when I go out to get the paper.

If you run into Bob and Ray together, it's a different matter. Over a year's time they must give away a million dollars worth of comedy material free to people they meet on the street.

Several years ago, I met them in New York after not having seen them for a long time. We said "hello" all the way around, but that was the end of any normal conversation.

"You still writing the Phil Rizzuto Show?" Ray asked, referring to a workaday sports talk show conducted by the former Yankee shortstop.

I laughed, but before I could think of any clever response, Bob stepped in.

"We don't get a chance to hear it much," he said.

"No, it comes at a bad time for us, Andy," Bob added. "What time is it on?"

"We hear you're doing a good job, though," Ray said.

"Yeah, everybody's talking about it."

I still hadn't gotten a word in when Ray finished the conversation.

"I'll bet the Scooter's a prince to work for, isn't he?"

"Great to see you, Andy. Keep up the good work," and they walked off.

The next time I saw them, they spotted me from across the street. Ray doubled over, pointed at me and started laughing. Ray is usually the instigator. Bob saw me. He pointed, doubled over and started laughing. They laughed for perhaps thirty seconds, then they straightened up and walked off down the street. It was the beginning and end of our meeting.

It was absolutely as meaningful as most street meetings, but for me a great deal more memorable.

If you bend double and laugh at the humor in situation comedies on television, you've just bought the wrong book. You're going to hate this one and if it isn't too late, take it back.

You'd be wrong if you did, though. I laugh out loud reading it. I look around for someone to read parts of it to. I find myself wondering why I'm laughing out loud, because laughing is something you normally do as a signal to someone else that you think a remark or a situation is funny. If I laugh alone over this book, who am I signaling? I think I'm trying to let Bob and Ray know how deeply they're appreciated by me. Their humor is so special, I'm afraid they'll think they're alone in the world with it.

Fortunately there are a lot of people who think, as I do, that they appreciate Bob and Ray more than anyone else does.

G. K. Chesterton said that not much art is produced by anyone who talks a lot about art. Not much humor is produced by anyone who talks a lot about what's funny, either. I've known Bob and Ray for twenty years, although I haven't seen them twenty times, and I've never heard them talk about humor. They just *are* funny. All the characters in their sketches are absolutely serious. The characters never let you know they think there's anything funny about what they're saying. Bob and Ray's humor isn't like a joke that depends on remembering the last line. Their sketches are just as funny in the middle as they are at the end.

I'm puzzled about what's funny and why some of us think one thing is funny and others don't. The question we don't seem able to resolve is whether things like humor, beauty, art or even broccoli strike us all the same or not. Does the difference lie in the way we respond to them, or in the way they strike us? If you eat all the broccoli on your plate and I leave all of mine, there's no way for either of us to know for sure whether it's because broccoli tastes different to you than it does to me, or because it tastes exactly the same but you like the taste and I don't. That's the way it is with humor but, unlike broccoli, I've never heard of anyone who ever listened to them who didn't like Bob and Ray.

Most of these sketches were originally done by Bob and Ray on radio. It's interesting to see how readily their spoken words adapt to the printed page. Nothing is lost and if you've ever heard them at all, you can hear every inflection in their voices as you read these words they spoke.

Contents

With a Cast of Literally Dozens, Including:

Roderick Ashford   Wally Ballou   Buddy Blodgett

Sanford Bluedorn   Victor J. Bodenhamer   Fahnstock P. Bodry

Leonard Bonfiglio   Biff Burns   David Chetley

Charley Chew   Judge Merton Claypool   Neil Clummer

Dr. Daryll Dexter   Fred Falvy   Edgar Fanshaw

Tillie Faunce   Ross Flecknoy   Ralph Flinger

Parnell W. Garr   Rex Grippner   Leonard P. Harkness

Harold the Baboon   Dr. Honeycutt   Martin LeSoeur

Nelson Malamon   Maitland W. Montmorency

The Murchfields   Alfred E. Nelson

John W. Norbis   Bodin Pardew   Millard L. Peevy

Hudley Pierce   Farley Plummer   Commander Neville Putney

Kid Quertus   Sgt. Ben Roister

Nurse Rudehouse   Big Fred Scoop   Clinton Snidely

Dr. Gerhard Snutton   Harlan Spivey, Jr.

Fabian Sturdley   Ralph Moody Thayer   Tippy, the Wonder Dog

Herbie Waitkus   Harlowe P. Whitcomb   Jasper Witherspoon

AND, OF COURSE,

King Zog

From Approximately

Coast to Coast ... It's

THE BOB AND RAY SHOW

The Bob and Ray Final Closeout Sale

RAY

Now . . . from approximately coast to coast . . . it's *The Bob and Ray Show!*

(*Theme: "Mention My Name in Sheboygan"*)

BOB

And it's all possible, thanks, in part to two of our old sponsors . . . Einbinder, the greatest name in flypaper. This year, more than ever before—make flypaper an important part of your life . . .

RAY

And by the Monongahela Metal Foundry . . . maker of shiny steel ingots. Monongahela—the metal foundry that casts its ingots with the housewife in mind!

BOB

And welcome again everybody—to the show and to some exciting news!

Because today, we announce our Bob and Ray Final Closeout, Absolute Clearance Sale!

RAY

We are being forced to vacate our premises! Our lease has been foreclosed!

BOB

Our landlord says we must go and his ultimatum is your good luck.

RAY

We have to get rid of every last piece of our tremendous stock at a ridiculous sacrifice!

BOB

Because we must go, you can buy men's two-pants suits for sixteen fifty. Men's three-pants suits for seventeen fifty. Men's four-pants suits for eighteen fifty-nine!

RAY

All men's *all*-pants suits for nineteen fifty! . . . You can get men's complete winter overcoats at twenty-two fifty, and men's winter overcoats—without sleeves—for seventeen fifty.

BOB

Our lease is up—and you get the benefit. Men's winter underwear with long legs and long sleeves for a dollar seventy-five. An extra pair of legs for only thirty-eight cents!

RAY

The landlord says "vacate" and that's it!
                    (Phone rings. Pickup)

RAY

Hello? Yes? What? We can? . . . Darn it!

BOB

What's the matter?

RAY

The landlord says we can stay another year!

(Organ: Playoff)

Wally Ballou Visits Sturdley House

RAY

This is the birthday of Fabian Sturdley, born in 1868 in Kenosha, Wisconsin . . . and our correspondent, Wally Ballou, is standing by with a report on what's happening at the birthplace of this famous American. He's at Sturdley House out there. It's a great tourist attraction, we're told, so . . . come in please, Wally Ballou . . .

BALLOU

——ly Ballou at "Driftwood," the stately old mansion where Fabian Sturdley was born, and I'm talking with his grandson, Van Tassel Sturdley, who manages this museum.

STURDLEY

Thanks, Mr. Ballou.

BALLOU

Is it true that the house has been restored to the original run-down condition it was in old Mr. Sturdley's time?

STURDLEY

Yes. They were going to tear down this grand old saltbox to make way for a combination car wash and bowling alley, but a group of public-spirited relatives banded together and have managed to save it, and have it declared a public shrine—with no taxes to pay!

BALLOU

Now, I know, of course, about Fabian Sturdley, but there may be some—especially children—who don't. Could you tell us something about your grandfather?

STURDLEY

Well, I'd say the big thing about him was eccentricity. For instance, he had electric lights in this house as far back as 1912—but because the neighbors laughed at him, he had them all taken out.

BALLOU

Replacing them with kerosene lamps, as the story goes. He took part in the Spanish-American War, I believe?

STURDLEY

Yes.

BALLOU

And upon his return he opened a puttee shop here?

STURDLEY

He was so impressed with the usefulness of puttees—convinced that civilians would want them for walking in tall grass—that he put all his money into his shop here, calling it "House of Puttees."

BALLOU

And it was in this very room that he held his famous meeting with Henry Ford in 1899.

STURDLEY

Mr. Ford came all the way out from Detroit to offer half interest in his company for ten thousand dollars. Of course, Grandpa realized that the automobile would never be more than a plaything for the wealthy . . . and he turned the offer down.

BALLOU

I was noticing a couple of other things visitors will see when they come here to fabulous Sturdley House . . . Here's a pillow that says, "Greetings from San Juan Hill."

STURDLEY

Yes, it's filled with balsam needles. It smelled nice for a while.

BALLOU

. . . An ash tray from Franconia Notch, New Hampshire . . . And what's the significance of that hole in the wall with a frame around it?

STURDLEY

That was when Grandfather shot at a traveling tinker and missed. He was moody that day because the bottom had fallen out of puttees. And there was a tight money situation, too.

BALLOU

Now, there's a kitchen out that way . . . and through this door a small den. I can see a pile of *National Geographics* and a picture of a blank Mount Rushmore. Not many of those around, I bet.

STURDLEY

It's a rare, valuable possession, yes.

BALLOU

Upstairs, there are two bedrooms and a bath.

STURDLEY

Yes, but they're roped off with a red velvet rope. That's where we live.

BALLOU

Do visitors get to see the attic?

STURDLEY

Yes. There are more *Geographics* up there—and about eleven cartons of puttees.

BALLOU

How about the basement?

STURDLEY

Down there they'll see our cat . . . and our trash cans . . . and several hundred cartons of puttees.

BALLOU

And outside, there's a small parking area.

STURDLEY

They can park on the street, too, as long as they don't block the Henshaws' driveway next door. The Henshaws don't like that!

BALLOU

Well, I'd like to thank you . . .

STURDLEY

Let me say that a visit to Sturdley House should be a must in anyone's vacation plans. We're open from nine to five. Admission is five dollars for adults, two dollars for children, and eighty-five cents for pets.

BALLOU

And if one were planning to stop here . . . how much time should they set aside to be sure to see everything?

STURDLEY

Including the vegetable garden out back?

BALLOU

Yes, and allowing about fifteen or twenty seconds to look at the bullet hole.

STURDLEY

I'd say . . . about . . . four and a half minutes.

BALLOU

Okay then, and thank you, Van Tassel Sturdley, grandson of Fabian Sturdley. Incidentally, when did he pass on?

STURDLEY

Grandpa?

BALLOU

Yes.

STURDLEY

Who said he died? He's downtown—getting a haircut!

BALLOU

Wally Ballou, then, at Sturdley House in Kenosha, Wisconsin, returning it to Bob and Ray!

Garish Summit—Episode #1

(Drama theme music. Establish and under for)

BOB

And now, Chapter One in the unfolding story of intrigue among the socially prominent families of Garish Summit. There—in stately splendor far removed from the squalid village below—they fight their petty battles over power and money.

(Theme up briefly and then fade for)

BOB

As our action begins, Miss Agatha is staring thoughtfully out the music room window. Suddenly, she turns and speaks . . .

AGATHA

There's a strange car stopping out in front, Rodney.

RODNEY

I wouldn't exactly call it strange, Mother. Of course, I never cared for rally stripes on a Rolls-Royce myself. However . . .

AGATHA

Oh, my word, Rodney! I don't mean strange in that sense. I just never saw it before. And now, a strange man is getting out.

RODNEY

I agree, Mother. He is an odd-looking duck. Ears set too low . . .

AGATHA

Oh, Rodney—you're such a wimp. You never understand a word I say to you.

(Doorbell)

RODNEY (Calls off)

Come in. It's open.
(Door opens and closes. Then a long period of footsteps)

RODNEY (Calls off)

Over here—in the music room.
(More footsteps. Then door opens and closes. Then more footsteps)

RODNEY (Calls off)

Back here—in the conversation pit behind the Wurlitzer.
(Another long period of footsteps)

MAN

Quite a place you've got here.

RODNEY

Thank you. We like it. We have forty-six thousand, two hundred square feet here in the main house. Then, the twins live over in the annex, which has . . .

AGATHA

Oh, shut up, Rodney. Whoever this man is, I'm sure he doesn't want to hear you recite a lot of boring figures.

RODNEY

You're quite right, Mother. Perhaps introductions would be more in order. I'm the wealthy but spineless young executive, Rodney Murchfield. And this is my dowager mother, Agatha.

MAN

Pleased to meet you, Miss Agatha. I've been looking forward to this moment. You see, I'm your long-lost elder son, Skippy.
(Organ: musical sting)

RODNEY

I'm afraid there's been some mistake, you sleazy impostor. I'm an only child and sole heir to the Murchfield billions. Mother, tell him you never had another son.

AGATHA

Well, I'm just trying to remember. That would have been about thirty years ago. And there were so many events going on at the country club then that it's hard to keep track of everything.

RODNEY

But, Mother—he's obviously feeding you a cock-and-bull story.

MAN

It's no cock-and-bull story, pal. I've got proof. Look! Here's a picture of me when I was four, and Mom took me to see Santa Claus at Gucci's.

RODNEY

What does this prove? There's no one in the picture but you and Santa Claus.

MAN

Well, of course not. A guy wouldn't want his mother in the picture when he was talking to Santa Claus.

RODNEY

Apparently you take me for a complete fool.

MAN

Yeah—more or less.

RODNEY

Well, I'm onto your little game. You fortune hunters are all alike. You learn how my Grandpa Murchfield was exploring for oil in this land in 1912 when he struck lead. It proved to be the Mother Lode—a rich vein of drab, gray metal stretching as far as the eye could see.

AGATHA

Oh, knock it off, Rodney. You always tell that story as if you had something to do with it.

RODNEY

Sorry, Mother. I guess I get carried away with family pride. After all, he was my grandfather.

MAN

Well, he was mine too. I remember he used to take me on his knee and say, "Skippy, someday it'll be your job to get the lead out."

RODNEY

He couldn't have said that to you. He died before you were born.

MAN

Oh, really? Well, maybe I heard it someplace else then.

RODNEY

Besides, no one in this family would ever have a name like Skippy.

AGATHA

Well, maybe that's just a nickname. His real name could be something more socially acceptable—like Caldwell or E. W.

RODNEY

Mother, believe me—this man's a fraud.

MAN

Caldwell sounds okay to me. Yep. No doubt about it. That's who I am— Caldwell Murchfield.

RODNEY

See, Mother? You're playing right into his hands.

AGATHA

No. I don't think so. I always liked the name Caldwell. But no one outside the family could have known that. It's good to have you home, Caldwell. Now come along and meet the others.

RODNEY

I wish you'd reconsider all this.

MAN

Oh, I already know part of the family, Mom. Like for instance Rodney's ravishingly beautiful wife, Jennifer. I know her well. Yes indeed. I know her real well! (*Evil chuckle*)

(*Organ: sting*)

BOB

Will this unknown man in the ready-to-wear suit be accepted as a Murchfield without any further questions? Can Jennifer provide some of the missing answers? And what about the butler who failed to answer the door when the stranger arrived? Perhaps we'll learn more next time when we hear Agatha say . . .

AGATHA

No. I didn't write you out of my will, Rodney. You were never in it.

BOB

That's next time when we resume our story of decadence as it unfolds on *Garish Summit.*

(*Organ: theme up briefly and then out*)

Hard Luck Stories

(Organ: sad background theme)

RAY

Again today our scouts have been searching the railroad and bus stations for victims of misfortune. We've found that you listeners enjoy hearing these pathetic people tell their tragic stories. And of course, we all get a warm feeling when our generous Bob and Ray organization steps forward with its lovely gifts to solve each and every problem. So Bob— let's start the fun with that sad specimen there beside you.

BOB

Sure thing, Ray. This is Mr. Morton Boatwright of Kansas City, Missouri. And according to your card, Mr. Boatwright—you became stranded in New York while you were attempting to begin a voyage to a virtually unexplored area of central Africa. I'm sure there must be quite a story that goes with that.

BOATWRIGHT

Well, no—at least not originally. I was just going to Africa because you can't buy a giraffe in Kansas City. But then, the tramp steamer I was planning to take from New York to the Ivory Coast left without me. And I've run out of money waiting around here for some other form of transportation. So I guess it has gotten to be quite an interesting story by now.

BOB

Yes. And I imagine it might become even more fascinating if we knew why you need a giraffe so badly.

BOATWRIGHT

Well, that's easy enough to explain. You see, I don't live right in Kansas City. I live in a suburb about twenty miles out of town. It's like most of your upper-middle-class suburbs where the neighbors all try to keep up with each other. One of them gets a new car—and then the rest of us have to. Next, one gets a boat—and then everybody else does. So I had to think of something that would really make the rest of them look shabby.

BOB

Like buying a giraffe, you mean.

BOATWRIGHT

That's right. It seemed like the ideal way to flaunt my wealth. A giraffe owner doesn't even have to mention that he's got a new giraffe. You just put him in the front yard and act casual about it, while the neighbors turn green with envy.

BOB

Well, it seems like a diabolical idea all right, Mr. Boatwright. But if you're only looking for a new way to flaunt your wealth—how do you happen to be appearing on our show as a hardship case?

BOATWRIGHT

My fried chicken franchise back home went bankrupt while I was hanging around here waiting for a tramp steamer to the Ivory Coast.

BOB

Well, then you truly merit our heartfelt sympathy, sir. But to help you get back on your feet, here's this lovely gift from our generous Bob and Ray organization. It's a gorgeous revolving lawn sprinkler complete with fifty yards of plastic garden hose.

BOATWRIGHT

Well, I can't flaunt this in front of the neighbors. They've already got sprinklers and garden hose.

BOB

That's perfectly all right. Just use it in good health . . . Now here with our next hard luck story is Mrs. Tillie Faunce of Logan, Utah. And I understand you're in desperate need of cash so you can walk clear across the country on your hands, Mrs. Faunce.

FAUNCE

That's right. I was quite a tomboy when I was a child. In fact, I was the only youngster who could walk clear across the school playground on her hands. So I guess that's why Tubby Wurtsma dee-double-dared me to walk all the way from New York to California on my hands. But it's taken me this long to scrape together even part of the money to start out.

BOB

Well, judging from your appearance, it must have been many years ago that you were a child. Do you think this little boy you spoke of still cares whether you accept his dare?

FAUNCE

Oh, indeed he does. It's gotten so I hate to go into his pinball arcade back home because I know he's going to make some smart remark about my failing to walk across the country on my hands. And I still may not be able to make it. I figure I'll wear out at least two hundred pairs of work gloves on the trip—and I can't afford to buy them.

BOB

Well, this is truly a terrible predicament in which you find yourself, Mrs. Faunce. But our generous Bob and Ray organization is standing by to help with this handsome gift. It's a chrome-plated head block for your hot rod from Conrad's Custom Cars of Cleveland.

FAUNCE

Well, I don't have a hot rod. Whatever gave you that idea?

BOB

That's quite all right, Mrs. Faunce. We're here to help . . . Now with today's final hard luck story, here is Mr. Farley Plummer of Tulsa, Oklahoma. And I understand you spent your life savings on a trip to New York to have some dental work done.

PLUMMER

That's right. As you may have noticed, I'm only ten-and-a-half inches tall. So, of course, I have a very small mouth and tiny little teeth in there. I couldn't find a dentist in Tulsa who had the right equipment to handle my case. So I figured I'd better come to a specialist in New York.

BOB

I see. And now you need the money to pay for a dental specialist here in New York to work on your teeth. Is that it?

PLUMMER

No. Now I need the money to go on to Dublin, Ireland. I found out there's no dentist in New York who specializes in people my size either. But one of them told me I'm about the same height as a leprechaun. And he assumed that those little guys all commute into Dublin to have their teeth fixed. So I want to give it a try. I've got one cavity that's really killing me.

BOB

Well, there's nothing more tragic to behold than the suffering of a fellow human—or whatever you are, sir. So from our generous Bob and Ray organization, here is this fine gift for you. It's a deluxe racing bike from Klingman and Klingman of Denver.

PLUMMER

Gee. I don't know what to say. Being ten-and-a-half inches tall, I get a lot of inappropriate gifts. But this really takes the cake.

BOB

No thanks are necessary, sir. Just seeing the smile on your little face is reward enough. And now back over to Ray at our main anchor desk.

(Organ: theme up to finish)

Slow Talkers of America

RAY

It's surprise time for me now, because I haven't had the opportunity to meet and talk to my next guest . . . Sit down, sir. Would you tell us your name and where you're from?

WHITCOMB

Harlowe . . . P. . . . Whitcomb . . .

RAY

Where are you from?

WHITCOMB

. . . from . . . Glens . . . Falls . . .

RAY

New York?

WHITCOMB

New . . . York.

RAY

What do you do?

WHITCOMB

I . . . am the . . . president . . . and recording . . .

RAY

Secretary? . . . Recording secretary?

WHITCOMB

. . . secretary . . . of . . . the S. . . . T. . . . O. . . . A. . . .

RAY

What does that stand for?

WHITCOMB

The . . . Slow . . . Talkers . . . of . . .

RAY

America.

WHITCOMB

America . . . We believe . . . in speaking slowly . . .

RAY

. . . So that you'll never be misunderstood!

WHITCOMB

. . . so that our ideas . . . our thoughts . . .

RAY

Words!

WHITCOMB

. . . and opinions . . .

RAY

Will never be misunderstood.

WHITCOMB

Will always . . . be . . .

RAY

Understood!

WHITCOMB

Understood. We . . . are . . . here . . .

RAY

In New York City.

WHITCOMB

. . . in New York . . . City . . . for our . . . annual . . .

RAY

Convention.

WHITCOMB

. . . membership . . .

RAY

Convention.

WHITCOMB

Convention. All . . . two hundred . . .

RAY

Members.

WHITCOMB

. . . and fifty . . .

RAY

Members!

WHITCOMB

. . . seven . . . members . . . speaking . . .

RAY

Slowly!!

WHITCOMB

. . . slowly. As opposed . . . to the members . . . of the . . . F. . . .

RAY

T. O. A.!

WHITCOMB

T. . . .

RAY

O. A.!!

WHITCOMB

O. . . .

RAY

A!!!!

WHITCOMB

A. The Fast . . .

RAY

Talkers of America!

WHITCOMB

Talkers . . .

RAY

Of America! You're making me a nervous wreck, sir!

WHITCOMB

Of . . .

RAY

Cut to a commercial . . . PLEASE!!!

WHITCOMB

America. We have a credo . . .

Monongahela Metal Foundry #1

RAY

A word to you ladies now, from our subscriber, the Monongahela Metal Foundry: Ladies, we don't expect you to take our word that Monongahela steel ingots are brighter and shinier than old-fashioned brands. Make a simple comparison test for yourself. Just drag one of your present ingots out in the yard on a sunny day and place it next to one of ours. If the Monongahela ingot doesn't shine more brightly— even without long hours of polishing—your money will be cheerfully refunded. Remember, too, ladies—you know how ashamed you feel serving dinner guests when there are dull, corroded steel ingots piled up on the table. That's why the folks at Monongahela have introduced new, extra shiny ingots for home and office use. You'll be proud to display them along with your finest china and silverware. Ask about them at your local Monongahela Foundry salesroom today.

BOB

Now . . . let me remind you that only two days remain to enter the giant sweepstakes contest now going on at your Monongahela Metal

Foundry. There's nothing to buy, and only a certain amount of obligation. But you could win a full new set of extra shiny ingots every month for as long as you live—or one of five hundred twenty-eight smaller prizes.

RAY

And the sweepstakes contest is so simple to enter. Just visit your local Monongahela dealer and give him your estimate of the total number. If your guess is close, you're a winner. But you must act before midnight tomorrow. So get on your thinking caps and start preparing your estimate now.

King Zog's Birthday

BOB

It's been said that some news might never occur if there were no microphones or television cameras to cover it; that events are often staged by pressure groups just to get some free air time. Editors can't know in advance whether a story is going to be real news—or just a media event. That was our problem when we handed out this assignment to reporter Artie Schermerhorn . . .

SCHERMERHORN

Here outside Oakdale Park we're awaiting the big protest rally that Albanian monarchists have scheduled for King Zog's birthday. This gentleman is one of the demonstrators . . .

DEMONSTRATOR

I don't think I should say anything before the others get here. Could you come back later?

SCHERMERHORN

No, I'm sorry. Your people were supposed to be staging a huge demonstration here an hour ago.

DEMONSTRATOR

Well, the others are coming over from Jersey in Bruno's Datsun. And you know us Albanians. We're always late.

SCHERMERHORN

Well, at least, tell us the purpose of this big protest you plan to stage—once the others get here.

DEMONSTRATOR

We're all of Albanian descent. And every year, we get together on King Zog's birthday and reminisce about the good old times.

SCHERMERHORN

And then you stage a demonstration in favor of restoring the monarchy. Is that it?

DEMONSTRATOR

No. Then we usually play pinochle. But this year we decided to try for some TV coverage. Only the guy in your newsroom said he wouldn't send a film crew out just to show us playing pinochle.

SCHERMERHORN

You really don't need to go into . . .

DEMONSTRATOR

He said it would only be visual if we got the whole mob together with picket signs. Then maybe the police would come and we'd have a pitched battle and . . .

SCHERMERHORN

Did our editor know that your whole membership could get into one car when he suggested that?

DEMONSTRATOR

I don't believe any specific numbers were mentioned—no.

SCHERMERHORN

I see. Well, now that you've gotten us down here, would you please pick up your sign and walk around with it?

DEMONSTRATOR

I'd feel kind of foolish doing it alone. Couldn't we wait till we're on the air?

SCHERMERHORN

We're on the air now, fellah.

DEMONSTRATOR

Oh, gosh. This is a real shame. Without the other guys here it may look like our group doesn't have much popular support.

SCHERMERHORN

I imagine it may look that way!

DEMONSTRATOR

Could you position your cameraman farther over, so I'll seem like a bigger crowd? You know, like the others are all standing behind me?

SCHERMERHORN

Look, Buster—I had a choice of two assignments today. And the one I turned down was a big ecology rally.

DEMONSTRATOR

Well, I wouldn't worry. Those people demonstrate at least once a week.

SCHERMERHORN

But today they were having Robert Redford. He was scheduled to do a sit-in next to a barrel of toxic chemical waste.

DEMONSTRATOR

I'm afraid you're a little naïve. I hear they always promise Robert Redford—but he usually doesn't even know about it.

SCHERMERHORN

Well, his name still draws a crowd. But I passed it up for you.

DEMONSTRATOR

And you won't be sorry. After all, there's nothing visual about a sit-in. For TV, you want people moving around. (*He picks up sign and starts walking in small circle*) Up with the monarchy! Albania for Albanians! Long live the monarchy!

SCHERMERHORN

And there you have it—the action at this moment from the potentially explosive rally at Oakdale Park. Now this is Artie Schermerhorn sending it back to our studio.

The Army Amateur Hour

(*Theme: Establish and under for*)

ROISTER
Hi. I'm Sergeant Ben Roister—and this is your Army Amateur Hour. Today, we're coming to you from Fort Armbrewster, Ohio—the home of the Fighting Three Hundred and Seventy-Ninth Horse-Drawn Infantry Brigade. Here on stage with me is our first contestant from Fort Armbrewster to compete for the coveted Drill Talent award. He's Corporal Edgar Balsh. Welcome to the show, Corporal.

BALSH
Thanks, Sergeant. And I'd just like to send a verbal greeting to all my buddies out there in the Forty-Sixth Hay Baling Unit of the Fighting Three Hundred and Seventy-Ninth Horse-Drawn Infantry Brigade.
(*Applause*)

ROISTER

Well, you've obviously got a lot of friends pulling for you today, Corporal. And I notice that you're now letting a lot of white mice out of their cages on top of the piano. Does that tie in somehow with the talent you're planning to display for us?

BALSH

Yes, it does, Sergeant. I have eighty-eight trained mice here. And of course, that figures out to one for each piano key. So as soon as they all get in position, I'll demonstrate how I've trained them to jump up and down in place—thereby creating a piano melody. (*Calls off*) Okay, you guys. Let's fall in line and count off there.

ROISTER

I see the mice are scampering around to find their places on the keyboard now. And while they're doing that, Corporal—suppose you tell us how they've been trained to jump up and down. Do they do it by voice command, or do you give the mice an electrical shock?

BALSH

Oh, it's strictly voice command, Sergeant. I'd never mistreat the little fellows, even though it's harder to train them using humane methods.

ROISTER

Well, it's admirable that . . .

BALSH

Excuse me, Sergeant—but I think they're all in place now. So I'd better get started while I still have their undivided attention.

ROISTER

Yes. By all means, go ahead. The stage is yours, Corporal Edgar Balsh.

BALSH

Okay, now. Let's look alert, fellows. One—two—three—and go!
(*Up tempo piano solo*)

BALSH (*Shouting*)

Six! Nine! Twelve! Forty-three! Pick up those feet, Number Five.

Okay. That's good. Just remember your numbers, guys. Good—good. You're a little slow there, Sixty-two. Jump higher, Fourteen. Higher. That's my boy. Good. Now you got it, fellas. Just keep it up. That's it.

(*Song plays to conclusion*)
(*Applause*)

ROISTER

Beautiful tune, Corporal—and really a great job of animal training. I'm sure we'll be seeing you in the district finals of our Drill Talent Award competition to be held in the Yale Bowl next February . . . Now, our next contestant this week on your Army Amateur Hour is Major Bertram Pudgeman. And I suppose your friends call you Bert.

PUDGEMAN

No. They call me Major Pudgeman. Of course, I don't have any really close friends.

ROISTER

Well, I'm sure we'd prefer not to hear about your problems in making friends. So why don't you tell us about the talent you've chosen to put on display here?

PUDGEMAN

Well, I do impersonations of famous military commanders in history. Quite a number of them became my heroes while I was at West Point. And I've worked up a little act built around my impressions.

ROISTER

Okay. That sounds like good clean entertainment. So the stage is all yours, Major Bertram Pudgeman.

PUDGEMAN

Well, first, here's my impression of a great favorite of mine—and I'm sure he's yours, too—General Mark Clark. (*Shouts*) To the rear, march . . . To the right flank, march . . . Forward, march. (*Lowers voice*) And that's all of him.

ROISTER

Okay. How about a nice round of applause for the major's impression of
General Mark Clark? *(Pause)* Well, I guess the men aren't going to
applaud. So you'd might as well go ahead, Major.

PUDGEMAN

Okay. Here's everybody's favorite from World War One—General
Black Jack Pershing. *(Shouts)* Fall in . . . Ten-shun! . . . At ease, men.
(Lowers voice) That's all I do on Pershing.
(Boos)

ROISTER

I don't think this is going over too well, Major. So maybe . . .

PUDGEMAN

It'll be okay. I'll get to my big finish—the hero of the Mexican War—
General Winfield Scott. *(Shouts)* Hup—two—three—four. Hup—two—
three—four. *(Lower voice)* That's it. I thank you.
(Boos)

ROISTER

I think you'd better duck out the back way before they tear you to
pieces, Major.

PUDGEMAN

Okay. I don't know what went wrong. My houseboy loved it.

ROISTER

And there he goes—our final contestant, Major Bertram Pudgeman . . .
And now this is Sergeant Ben Roister saying so long until next time,
when we'll be coming your way from the Exeter, New Hampshire,
Marine Base—home of the Battling Fourteenth. See you then.

(Theme up and out)

Ambiguous Signs

BOB

One of the big problems facing our towns and cities these days seems
to be finding new ways to raise revenues—to get money to keep these
towns and cities running. We've come across a gentleman who has a
very unusual business, and a very successful one, too. It's a service
business. He supplies these municipalities with what he calls "ambiguous
signs." He's Mr. Edgar Fanshaw . . . Is that a fairly reasonable description of your job that I gave?

FANSHAW

Yes, that was fine. I'd like to add a few additional words if I may.
Most towns and communities have reached the saturation point in taxa-
tion. That is, real estate taxes, school taxes, and so forth. And yet they
have an ever increasing need for monies to keep the town operating.
So that's where we at the sign company come in. We make ambiguous

signs, signs that are so difficult to understand that they are easily violated. Hence communities can assess fines for these violations.

BOB

I see. The fines are where they get this needed revenue.

FANSHAW

That's true. Yes. Now, I have brought some signs along with me. Here, now this first ambiguous sign is a beauty. We're very proud of it. It's a fifty-dollar violation in most communities.

```
┌─────────────────────────────┐
│                             │
│     DON'T NOT MAKE          │
│                             │
│       LEFT TURN             │
│                             │
│        EXCEPT               │
│                             │
│         7–10                │
│                             │
│          5–8                │
│                             │
└─────────────────────────────┘
```

BOB

That would take some time to figure out.

FANSHAW

By the time the motorist figures that sign out he would get another ticket for obstructing traffic. Now this next one has a trick in it. My boy, Leland, came up with this one. See if you can spot it.

```
┌───────────────────────┐
│                       │
│     QUIET ZONE        │
│      EXCEPT           │
│     TUES AND          │
│      THRUS            │
│                       │
└───────────────────────┘
```

BOB

I'm good at these things. I spotted that right away. The abbreviation for Thursday is misspelled. There's no such thing as "Thrus" . . .

FANSHAW

That's right. The only day you can be noisy there is Tuesday. This next one is a year round money-maker. Thirty-dollar violation for this one.

```
+-----------------------+
|                       |
|      OFFICIAL         |
|                       |
|       SNOW            |
|                       |
|      STREET           |
|                       |
+-----------------------+
```

FANSHAW

It's as bad to be there in August as it is in February.

BOB

I believe you told me you have one that works in a public service message?

FANSHAW

Yes. We like to think we have a heart over at the Ambiguous Sign Company. This next one is our attempt at a public service. We have a health message here. See if you can spot it.

```
+-----------------------+
|                       |
|     FIRE  LANE        |
|                       |
|        NO             |
|                       |
|     SMOKING           |
|                       |
+-----------------------+
```

FANSHAW

We are very proud of that one. This next one is our second biggest money-maker. It's very popular in most communities.

```
┌─────────────────────────────┐
│                             │
│            NO               │
│                             │
│          PARKING            │
│                             │
│         ON TOP 8–4          │
│                             │
│       NO STANDING 4–12      │
│                             │
│         NO PARKING          │
│                             │
│           TODAY             │
│                             │
│                             │
└─────────────────────────────┘
```

BOB

That would certainly drive me up the wall!

FANSHAW

Most motorists, by the time they get to the "NO PARKING TODAY"
are so frustrated that they leave their vehicle and start to kick the sign.
There, again, they get another ticket for destroying public property.

BOB

And of course you get more reorders for the signs they've destroyed.

FANSHAW

That's true. Yes. Glad you mentioned that. Now, with the Federal
Highway Program in full gear, most communities now have freeways
that go from one end of town to the other, speeding the traffic flow.
Well, now, that presented a particularly knotty problem for my son
and myself till we came up with a set of three sequential signs. Here's
the first one.

```
┌─────────────────────────────┐
│                             │
│       EXIT 7 ½ MILE         │
│                             │
└─────────────────────────────┘
```

BOB

That looks fairly normal.

FANSHAW

Yes it does. Now look at this one.

```
EXIT 7 ¼ MILE
```

FANSHAW

Now here's where we get them for a one-hundred-and-fifty-dollar fine.

```
EXIT 7 CLOSED
NO TURNS
```

General Pharmacy

(Dramatic organ music)

BOB

Welcome now to *General Pharmacy*—the dramatic story of handsome young druggist Ross Flecknoy—and his struggle to save humanity at the prescription counter of a pharmacy still technically owned by his aging father.

(Theme up briefly and then fade for)

BOB

As our scene opens today, Ross is carefully buttoning his pharmaceutical smock to begin work—when suddenly a stranger he has never seen before approaches the prescription counter.

ASHFORD

Good morning. I know you've never seen me before—but I'm sure you recognize me from my pictures. I'm Roderick Ashford, star of stage, screen, and television. My lovely wife—the former Brenda Hume—has recently left me for another man. So now I need this prescription filled.

FLECKNOY

I'm afraid you'll have to wait a moment. I'm still buttoning my pharmaceutical smock to begin work.

ASHFORD

Very well. But I'm sure I don't need to tell you—it's rather urgent.
(Sound: Running footsteps approaching)

FAPP

Hey, Mr. Ashford! What a break finding you here! Remember me? Eddie Fapp, cub reporter for the old *Hollywood Evening Graphic*.

ASHFORD

No. I don't remember you. And what's more, I have nothing to say to the press about the status of my on-again-off-again marriage to the lovely Brenda Hume.

FLECKNOY

Okay. I can fill your prescription now, Mr. Ashford.

ASHFORD

Just say I'll always remember Brenda as she was when I first picked her out of the back row of a chorus line and made her my wife.

FAPP

Oh, that's a great quote, Mr. Ashford. You know, getting this scoop could be a big turning point for me at the *Evening Graphic*. I sure hope so. Trying to support my chronically ill mother on a salary of only forty-two dollars a week has been rough.

ASHFORD

Well, I'm afraid I have nothing to say that would make a headline, son. Naturally, I miss Brenda desperately. But as the idol of the nation's women, I don't suppose I'll ever be lonely.

FAPP

The doctors say an operation might help Mom. But they don't promise anything. And on my salary, it's out of the question anyway.

ASHFORD

Even so, I'll probably dispose of the big house up in the hills. Eighteen rooms is too much for a man alone to look after.

FLECKNOY

If you've lost the prescription, I can call the doctor and get it again. That's one of the humanitarian things I often do.

ASHFORD

And, of course, every one of those rooms shall forever remain filled with memories of Brenda.

FAPP

Mom fell on the ice and broke her hip about five years ago. That was the start of the whole thing. Being bedridden just seems to leave a person open to all kinds of infection.

ASHFORD

I imagine I'll spend more time at the cottage in Palm Springs now. I've neglected my golfing because Brenda never liked the game.

FAPP

Just lying in bed that long weakens the lungs. And now Mom seems to look a litle worse every night when I come home from the office.

ASHFORD

I've neglected so many things because Brenda didn't like them. All I cared about was pleasing Brenda.

FAPP

I think I'd give the operation a try even if the doctors can't promise anything. But on forty-two dollars a week, it's out of the question.

ASHFORD

You'd think that would mean something to her, wouldn't you?

FAPP

Oh, it would mean the world to her. But I just can't swing it.

ASHFORD

Yes. I guess that's become the story of my life now—I just can't swing it.

FLECKNOY

I'm afraid I'll have to fill somebody else's prescription first if you won't give me yours.

ASHFORD

That's quite all right. You can take this gentleman ahead of me.

FAPP

Oh, I haven't got a prescription. On forty-two dollars a week, I can't afford one.

ASHFORD

Strangely enough, I find that understandable. I've never said this publicly—but I was once poor myself. And now that the secret is out, I can't tell you how much better I feel.

(Theme)

BOB

And so, handsome young druggist Ross Flecknoy continues aiding those who come to him in search of prompt relief. But what dark clouds may be hovering on the horizon for Ross? Be sure to join us tomorrow when we'll hear lovely Brenda Ashford say . . .

BRENDA

But I don't understand. I thought all aspirin was alike.

BOB

That's in the next dramatic episode of . . . *General Pharmacy.*

(Theme up briefly and then out)

Biff Burns's Sports

B U R N S

Greetings and the warmest of felicitations to you, sports fans. This is Biff Burns emanating from mikeside here in the Biff Burns Sports Room. In the moments that lie directly ahead, we shall be scrutinizing all the highlights and sidelights from the world of sports. In addition, we'll be chatting with one of the truly dominant figures in sports, Edgar Barnhorst. And Edgar—suppose we begin with a most penetrating question: What have you ever done to become a truly dominant figure in sports?

B A R N H O R S T

Well, it's really not what I've done so far, Biff. It's what I'm about to do. I'm going to end all the legal fights over contracts and salaries that professional athletes have been getting into lately with the team owners.

BURNS

Well, I'm sure that such an achievement would indeed be hailed by all the leaders of the sporting fraternity, including myself. But how do you propose to keep sports stars from getting into contract disputes with team management, Edgar?

BARNHORST

Well, I've got an ingenious idea for doing that, Biff. You see . . .

BURNS

Excuse me for interjecting, Edgar. But before you begin, I'd just like to say that this is my show. And therefore, I'll make the decision as to whether your idea is ingenious or not.

BARNHORST

Oh, sure, Biff. I didn't mean to be stepping over into your territory. But I'm sure you'll think the idea is pretty ingenious. You see, I plan to change the rules for all sports so they'll be a lot easier to play. Then, athletes won't have the nerve to demand so much money because they'll know they're not doing anything very difficult.

BURNS

Well, that may or may not be an ingenious idea, Edgar. It all depends upon what you're talking about when you infer that sports will be easier to play under your proposed rules.

BARNHORST

Well, I think basketball is a good example of what I'm talking about, Biff. Right now, you've got young guys just out of school squabbling with management over million-dollar contracts. And the only reason they're able to ask for that kind of money is because they're seven feet tall—but they're still graceful and able to move around well.

BURNS

Well, with all due respect, Edgar, I don't see how you propose to make a young man more clumsy if he has a natural tendency to be graceful.

BARNHORST

Well, I think you'll see that's now what I'm proposing to do if you'll just clam up and let me explain the thing, Biff. You see, under my rules, the basket will be lowered about two feet. And guys will be allowed to run with the ball if they want to. And we may also make the basket bigger around so it'll be easier to score. That way, I figure any middle-aged man standing five-feet-six should have enough talent to play pro ball.

BURNS

I see. And if this idea of yours proves to be as ingenious as you think— this will cut down on unreasonable salary demands in the N.B.A.

BARNHORST

Well, sure it will, Biff. How can a guy demand a million bucks when he knows that almost every man in the country under the age of sixty is able to play as good as he does?

BURNS

Well, that does indeed have all the superficial earmarks of being an ingenious idea, Edgar.

BARNHORST

Thanks. I believe my new rules may have an even bigger impact on major league baseball. There, I plan to make the ball a lot bigger and softer—kind of like a volleyball. Test results indicate that it'll take a lot less talent to play in the major leagues under those conditions.

BURNS

I assume the ball will be easier to hit, and also to field, if it's large and soft.

BARNHORST

That's right. As I say, I've got test results on that, Biff. We tried the proposed equipment in a Little League in my home town last season. And even the worst hitter batted nine twenty-seven. So I don't see how Rod Carew could ask for more than a couple of hundred dollars a week—knowing that any eight-year-old kid can play ball as good as he does.

BURNS

Well, that's a fascinating concept for the imagination to toy with, Edgar.

BARNHORST

Thanks, Biff. Coming from you, that means more than it would normally.

BURNS

I suppose that's true. But there's one question that I continue tossing over in my mind. Why would the fans pay money to come out and watch sports that don't require any playing skill?

BARNHORST

Well, I think the fans are going to have to lower their standards—and stop expecting to see professional athletes who have talent.

BURNS

I see. And do you expect the fans to cooperate by lowering their standards that way?

BARNHORST

No. I don't think they'll do that, Biff.

BURNS

I don't think they will, either. But thanks for stopping by to tell us about your impractical idea. And now this is Biff Burns saying that until time for our next get-together in the sports room, this is Biff Burns saying so long, fans.

Mr. District Defender

RAY

Now, let us join Mr. District Defender—champion of the weak and the helpless.

(Establish and under for documentary type theme. Organ)

MR. D. D.

I am the city's district defender. It's my job to defend the weak and the helpless as they come into daily contact with the parasites of society that lurk all around us. Any decent person could easily fall victim to the con man—the grifter—the hoaxster. All I can do is stand ready to wage war against evil from my office high atop the old Van Brewster Building. It was there that my latest heartbreaking case began . . .

(Organ: out)

LADY

Now wait a minute, Harold. Don't go trotting around like a chicken

with its head cut off. I'll bet maybe this nice-looking young man could
help us.

MR. D. D.

I'm sure I could, dear lady. You and this man—whom I judge to be
your husband—look like natural targets of the con man—the grifter—
the hoaxster. Please sit down and tell me all about it.

MAN

Well, I really don't know whether we ought to take up your time. As
I was telling Martha on the way down here—there are some winners
in life and some born losers. So maybe we ought to just write off this
whole thing and forget it.

MR. D. D.

Well, I can appreciate how you feel, sir. Nobody likes to admit that
he's been a gullible fool. But as the district defender, I'm here to
help. So just tell us your story from the beginning.

LADY

Well, Harold's been a gullible fool, Mr. District Defender.

MR. D. D.

Yes. I'm sure he has. But I'd already guessed that for myself. So suppose you go back and tell me your story from the beginning.

LADY

Well, Harold and I operate a small greasy spoon restaurant on the
outskirts of the city. It's what they call a mom and pop establishment—
even though we have no children of our own.

MR. D. D.

I get the picture, and a tragic one it is. Decent people like yourselves
are easy marks for the con man—the hoaxster—the grifter. But please
go on.

LADY

Well, about a week ago, a man came in and asked if he could get change
for a ten-dollar bill to use the telephone.

MR. D. D.

How tragically familiar this all sounds—the old change-a-big-bill-to-use-the-phone gimmick. Did you bring along the counterfeit ten he gave you so that I can enter it in evidence?

MAN

No. We didn't do that. In fact, I think we've already taken up too much of your time with this.

MR. D. D.

Please—let me be the judge of that. It's little people like yourselves who must step forward if these hoaxsters are to be stopped. But too many victims are ashamed to admit that they behaved like complete idiots. So just continue with your story.

LADY

Well, at first, I didn't want to give the man change unless he at least ordered a cup of coffee or something. But Harold foolishly gave him change for a ten—and the man went to the phone.

MR. D. D.

Then, I'm sure he quickly pretended to get a busy signal so he could duck out before you had time to examine the bill.

LADY

No. As a matter of fact, he had quite a long conversation. And he seemed to be talking to a stock broker.

MR. D. D.

Of course—of course. The old phony-stock-broker-on-the-other-end trick. And I suppose you both became so fascinated with his conversation that you failed to notice he hadn't given you a genuine ten-dollar bill.

LADY

No. Harold tells me now that he noticed that almost as soon as the man turned away from the counter with his change.

MR. D. D.

I understand it all quite clearly now. Your husband kept silent because law-abiding citizens don't realize that counterfeiters seldom resort to crimes of violence when they're caught. It was fear that kept you from shouting at the man when you realized he'd given you a counterfeit ten-dollar bill. Right, sir?

MAN

No. I guess it was just shock. You see, he hadn't given me a counterfeit ten. He'd accidentally given me a genuine hundred-dollar bill— but I only gave him change for ten.

MR. D. D.

You say he gave it to you accidentally? Sir, I'm afraid you still don't understand how the con man preys on his victim by handing out large denomination bills. And I suppose you permitted him to go away without even letting him know that you'd discovered his trick.

MAN

Yeah. Judging from his conversation with the stock broker—I figured he had plenty of money. And nobody'd ever know the difference. But of course, when Martha added up the receipts at the end of day, they didn't balance. We were ninety dollars over.

MR. D. D.

But by then—needless to say—the man who had victimized you was long gone. And you were left with only a hazy recollection of what he looked like.

LADY

Well, I'd say I got a pretty good look at him. And I thought maybe you could help us find a man answering his description so we could give the money back and balance our books. He was about six-feet-four-and-a-half—weight 214—hair that was blond and wavy on one side, but black and straight on the other—lavender eyes—part of the ring finger missing from the left hand—a mole on the end of his nose—and he was wearing blue ear muffs.

MR. D. D.

I'm sorry, dear lady—but do you have any idea how many men are walking the streets of this city wearing blue ear muffs? We'd never find him. All I can say is that you've been taken. But I hope this experience will teach you a lesson—and that you will never again need the help of . . . Mr. District Defender.

(*Organ: Theme up and out*)

Forbush Dinnerware

BOB

Folks—Bob and Ray are in trouble, and we're going to ask you to help us out.

RAY

Yes, folks—we're in trouble, and we're going to ask you to help us out.

BOB

We have in our Overstocked Warehouse, exactly two thousand four hundred and thirty-six sets of Forbush Dinnerware. Forbush Dinnerware—the plates a nation eats off. Of.

RAY

Our accountants tell us we're crazy. They say we are absolutely stark raving mad to have so many sets of Forbush Dinnerware in our warehouse.

BOB

They tell us we gotta unload them! We've gotta get them out of that warehouse in *five days*! So, do you know what we're going to do? We're going to unload these two thousand four hundred and thirty-six sets of Forbush Dinnerware at such a low, low price that *you* will say we're crazy, too!

RAY

But we're going to take that risk. Maybe we *are* crazy, but we're going to unload these sets of Forbush Dinnerware *no matter how big a loss we take*! Our accountants say they've gotta go—and they've gotta go!

BOB

You folks all know Forbush Dinnerware—the plates a nation eats off of. We have two thousand four hundred and thirty-six sets of them, and we're going to practically *give* them away at such a low, low price that you'll say "Bob and Ray are crazy!"

RAY

But—we're going to take that chance. Now listen to this terrific, crazy offer. Two thousand four hundred and thirty-six sets of Forbush Dinnerware for only *one dollar and ninety-eight cents*!!

BOB

Now you *know* we're crazy! Genuine Forbush Dinnerware! Of course, at this crazy price, every set is not identical. Some sets have forty-eight pieces—some sets forty-six pieces—some sets have forty-two and a half pieces. And, naturally, sets are not all of the same color. Some have gold and pink plates with orange creamer, blue gravy boat, and iridescent yellow cups and saucers. But *every color* is the true Forbush baked-on, guaranteed color.

RAY

And, of course, at this low, low crazy price, every piece is not absolutely *whole*. Some pieces may have slight cracks imperceptible to the eye. Some may have a handle missing, or a small piece out of the bottom. But every break is a *clean break*, and bears the Forbush seal of approval.

BOB

Be the first in your neighborhood to have a set of Forbush California Dinnerware. "California" means, of course, *unmatched*, a rage that is sweeping the country. Set your table with yellow, pink, magenta, and mottled green plates; red, white, and blue cups and saucers. Be gay! Be mad! Be modern!

RAY

Be the first in your neighborhood to have a set of Forbush Carefree Dinnerware. "Carefree" means, of course, slightly chipped, cracked, or broken. A gravy boat with no handle makes a real conversation piece. A soup tureen with a hole in its side sets a really gay, carefree mood for dinner.

BOB

So folks: We ask you to help out two crazy guys who have just one thought in mind: to bring happiness into your homes. Help us unload these two thousand four hundred and thirty-six sets of Forbush Dinnerware at a crazy price.

RAY

Just send us a dollar ninety-eight.

BOB

And if you do . . . you're crazy, too!

Mr. I-Know-Where-They-Are

RAY

Now, we're in for another nostalgic interlude, as we welcome Ralph Flinger to our microphone. Ralph is better known to most of you as Mr. I-Know-Where-They-Are. He's spent a lifetime tracking down old-time celebrities who are no longer in the spotlight. And Ralph, it's amazing how many of our listeners write in asking your help as they try to locate their favorites of days gone by.

FLINGER

Well, I'm delighted to do whatever I can to help, Ray. You know, I send out more than a hundred birthday cards on the average day to washed-up celebrities who have grown a year older. And I know it makes them feel better when I can include a little note that tells them they're still remembered by your listeners.

RAY

Well, they certainly are remembered, Ralph. And this letter I have right here from a woman in Oregon is typical of those that come in addressed to Mr. I-Know-Where-They-Are. She says that her girlhood hero was a rich society playboy named Wainbridge Van Cortlant. But she hasn't read anything about him in the paper for years. And she wonders whatever became of him.

FLINGER

Oh, for goodness' sakes alive—Wainbridge Van Cortlant. His grand-father made millions selling defective railroad ties back in the nine-teenth century when the Iron Horse was first spanning the country.

RAY

And tying it together into one great nation, you mean.

FLINGER

Yes—except on the lines where Old Man Van Cortlant had provided the railroad ties. The wood in most of them was infested with termites. So that caused the locomotives to tip over before they had a chance to tie this country together into one great nation.

RAY

I see. But of course, Wainbridge Van Cortlant wasn't responsible for any of that.

FLINGER

Oh, no. That swindle of his grandfather's happened long before his time. About the worst thing Wainbridge ever did was ride down Wall Street during the Depression on one of his polo ponies. Several former stockbrokers were kicked as they stood on the sidewalk trying to sell apples. But later, Wainbridge gave them each a dollar to show that it was nothing personal.

RAY

Well, it sounds as if he was a decent sort of a fellow that any young girl might have worshiped from afar. But where is he now?

FLINGER

Well, Wainbridge lost everything during the war, Ray. He'd invested the family fortune in buying a South Pacific island. But the Japanese managed to sink it some way. I think they just let the air out underneath it, and it fell. Anyway, Wainbridge now lives in a small furnished room across the street from the bus station in St. Louis. He supports himself by raising goldfish and selling them to neighbors.

RAY

Well, that's quite a comedown for a millionaire playboy. But at least you've answered the lady's question . . . Now our next letter addressed to Mr. I-Know-Where-They-Are is from a man in Utah. He remembers a famous rodeo rider of years ago named Tumbleweed Gargon. And he wonders if you happen to know where Tumbleweed is now.

FLINGER

Oh, indeed I do know where Tumbleweed Gargon is, Ray. I think he was a hero of every young fellow who grew up in the West. He used to rope wild bison before that rodeo event was outlawed by most state legislatures.

RAY

Well, that's interesting. Where is Tumbleweed now?

FLINGER

I don't think they ever officially outlawed bison roping in Montana. But since the event had been dropped from rodeos in other states, it gradually died out in Montana, too.

RAY

I see. Well, what about Tumbleweed Gargon? Where is he now?

FLINGER

A lot of people claimed that bison roping constituted cruelty to animals. I don't know why. They still have calf roping in rodeos. And calves are similar to bison, except that they're not as woolly.

RAY

Yes. I guess that's true. But where is Tumbleweed Gargon now?

FLINGER

He's in Fort Worth, Texas.

RAY *(After a pause)*

Is that all?

FLINGER

Yes. As far as I know.

RAY

Okay. Then I guess that takes care of that . . . Now, we have time for just one more quick question addressed to Mr. I-Know-Where-They-Are. It's from a woman in Virginia. And she's wondering about a former child movie star named Fat Baby Moxford. She thinks he was a member of the group that called themselves the Little Cut-Ups.

FLINGER

Yes. Not many people remember that—but Fat Baby Moxford was one of the original Little Cut-Ups. He was later replaced by Pinky Luling. The studio had to drop Fat Baby around 1927 because he stopped being a baby, even though he did manage to remain fat.

RAY

Well, that should give the listener who wrote in a lot of good background information. But what she really wants to know is whatever became of Fat Baby Moxford.

FLINGER

Well, he's now the president of a large corporation in Palo Alto, California, that deals in computer software, Ray. And I think that's really quite a tribute to his ability. I imagine it's hard for a middle-aged man to get to the top in the business world when his name is Fat Baby Moxford.

RAY

Yes. I'm sure he'd have to put forth extra effort to prove that he had what it took—particularly in computer software. So just let me thank you for answering the lady's question—and also those of our other listeners.

FLINGER
I was delighted to do it, Ray. Just chatting about all these old people helps keep me young. Good-bye.

Einbinder Flypaper #1

RAY

Say . . . here's good news for the busy gift shopper! Do you have trouble selecting just the right present for Christmas, birthdays, and other special occasions? Then why not offer the token of love and esteem that's welcomed by all—a gift certificate for Einbinder Flypaper? They're available in denominations of ten, fifty, and one hundred dollars.

BOB

And they can be redeemed for whichever size and style of flypaper best suits the needs of the recipient. Friends will love you for your thoughtfulness. And they'll also admire your good taste in selecting a gift certificate for genuine Einbinder Flypaper—the brand you've gradually grown to trust over the course of three generations!

Garish Summit—Episode #2

(Dramatic theme music: Establish and under for)

BOB

Welcome again to Garish Summit and its endless story of intrigue among the socially prominent. There—in stately splendor far removed from the squalid village below—the beautiful people fight their petty battles over power and money.
(Theme up briefly and then fade for)

BOB

As our action begins, strong-willed Agatha Murchfield is in the solarium, awaiting the arrival of her lawyer, Bodin Pardew.
(Door opens and closes. Then footsteps)

AGATHA

Is that you, Bodin?

PARDEW

Yes. I seem to be somewhere in the entry hall, Agatha. Can you talk me in from here?

AGATHA

Just hang a right through the music room and then cut across the west edge of the library until you get to the solarium. You can't miss it.

PARDEW

Very well. I'm on my way.
(*About ten seconds of footsteps. The door opens and closes. Then more prolonged footsteps. Then another door opens and closes*)

AGATHA

Ah, there you are, Bodin. It's been ages.

PARDEW

Yes it has, Agatha. But that's only because the carpet cleaners had the library blocked, and I had to double clear back through the dining room . . . I must say you're looking well, except that you seem drawn and haggard—as if you haven't slept in days.

AGATHA

Well, I have something preying on my mind that I need your help with, Bodin. A man has turned up here in Garish Summit who claims to be my long-lost elder son, Caldwell.

PARDEW

That's shocking, Agatha. We've known each other for forty years, and I always thought your weak-willed son, Rodney, was an only child.

AGATHA

Well, I thought so, too. That's the strange part I don't understand.

PARDEW

Well, you're a fabulously rich widow who's inherited the world's largest chain of lead mines. The man's probably a fortune hunter.

AGATHA

No. I've encountered those before. But this chap definitely claims to be the son I never knew I had. So, of course, it's just his word against mine.

PARDEW

Well, I'm not sure that's the case. But how can I be of help?

AGATHA

I want you to check out his story, Bodin. See if there's a birth certificate—look into hospital records—dig through newspaper files . . . Well, aren't you going to write down these instructions?

PARDEW

I suppose I could, if you like. The back of this envelope is blank, so all I need is a point on my pencil. Is there a sharpener around anywhere, Agatha?

AGATHA

Over there under the window by the tumbling mat.

PARDEW

Thank you. I'll be back in a jiffy.
            (*Prolonged footsteps, then the grinding of a pencil sharpener. A pause. Then more grinding of the sharpener*)

AGATHA

My stars, Bodin! What are you doing over there?

PARDEW

It's all right, Agatha. Everything's being taken care of.
            (*More pencil sharpening. Then footsteps*)

PARDEW

There, now. Shall we begin?

AGATHA

Well, first, I want to find out whether a birth certificate was ever issued for a Caldwell Murchfield. Then . . .

PARDEW

Just a minute. *(Mumbles to himself)* She—wants—me—to—find—out . . .

AGATHA

My word! How did a nincompoop like you ever get to be my attorney?

PARDEW

I don't know, Agatha. I suppose I could look in the files at my office
and see if I have any documents covering that.

AGATHA

No. Don't waste any more time. Just find out if this mysterious stranger
is really my eldest son. If he is, I'll want to rewrite my will to exclude
my other boy, Rodney.

PARDEW

I understand. Incidentally, about this young man who calls himself
Caldwell Murchfield. Where is he now?

AGATHA

Rodney took him moose hunting. Caldwell had wanted to go to the
bank and rummage through my safe deposit box. But Rodney insisted
they go hunting first.

PARDEW

Were both young men carrying shotguns when they left here, Agatha?

AGATHA

No. I remember that part distinctly because it struck me as strange.
Rodney had a gun, but he told Caldwell just to carry a shovel.

PARDEW

Agatha, I think this has the makings of a dangerous situation.

AGATHA

Well, I told them that before they left. You can't bring down a moose
with a shovel. But Rodney said not to worry. He said there's no space
in the trophy room for another stuffed animal, anyway!

PARDEW

I'm afraid this is no longer a case for a lawyer. I'm going to call the police.

(Musical stinger)

AGATHA

Well, I guess the police couldn't botch things up any worse than you always do. But will they hunt for those old birth records I need?

PARDEW

A more urgent matter is involved here, Agatha. To put it as delicately as possible—one of your sons may have slaughtered the other.

(Theme. Establish and under for)

RAY

Must Agatha now face the loss of a son that she had assumed was lost all along? Can Caldwell be a murder victim if birth records show that he never existed? And what about the blank envelope that Bodin Pardew mysteriously found in his pocket? Perhaps we'll learn more next time when we hear Rodney Murchfield say . . .

RODNEY

I know it's only a raccoon. But I thought pasting these horns on its head might make it seem like more.

RAY

That's next time when we resume our story of wealth and intrigue on *Garish Summit.*

(Theme up briefly and then out)

Buddy Blodgett at the Polygon Ballroom

RAY

Now we've come up to music time here on the old Bob and Ray Show. So for your afternoon listening pleasure, let's swing out to the Polygon Ballroom in Larchmont for the haunting melodies of Herbie Waitkus and his orchestra.

(Finish of Glenn Miller's "In the Mood")
(Applause)

BLODGETT *(Jovial)*

Yes, indeed—indeed. This is Buddy Blodgett speaking to you from the old Polygon Ballroom in Larchmont, where dozens of sailors on leave have gathered to dance with the local girls and listen to the music of Herbie Waitkus and his orchestra. Now, I see that Herbie is again raising his baton. So here's another foot-tapping tune played in the distinctive Herbie Waitkus style.

(A few bars of Tijuana Brass)
(Applause)

BLODGETT

Indeed—indeed. Herbie Waitkus and his fine orchestra with another of those short renditions that are so familiar in dime-a-dance joints like the Polygon Ballroom. And now, as the boys in the band take a short break, we're moving across the dance floor with our equipment to chat with the maestro. Greetings and welcome to our Bob and Ray microphone.

WAITKUS *(Very suspicious)*

Who are you and what do you want?

BLODGETT

I'm Buddy Blodgett. And we're beaming the haunting melodies of your orchestra out across the air lanes to our Bob and Ray audience.

WAITKUS

Well, I sure wasn't told about this. So I'd suggest you pack up your junk and get out of here.

BLODGETT

Well, I'm sorry, Herbie. But this pickup has been cleared with the management of the old Polygon Ballroom here in downtown Larchmont. And I'm certainly not going to leave after we've paid to have our lines run in here.

WAITKUS

Well, then get over to the other side of the room someplace where you won't be under my feet. Okay?

BLODGETT

Well, I certainly don't think our Bob and Ray microphone will be in your way. And I'd just like to talk a little bit about your group's distinctive style before . . .

WAITKUS

Look pal—I've got no time to talk to you about anything right now. The guys are getting back on the bandstand, and the customers pay to get music. So just buzz off. Understand?

BLODGETT

Well, I must say that your personality is a little different from the type we find among most popular band leaders, Herbie. But we can chat about that later.

WAITKUS

Don't count on it. Now just get out of the way, and let us do what we're getting paid for. I don't want to have to get rough with you.

BLODGETT

Well, we're in complete agreement on that. And I was just stepping aside so our audience can hear another haunting melody played in the distinctive Herbie Waitkus style.
(A few bars of David Rose's "Holiday for Strings")
(Applause)

BLODGETT

Indeed—indeed. The melodic "Holiday for Strings" rendered by Herbie Waitkus and his orchestra. And now, as we move back to the bandstand to resume our chat with the maestro, I have just one question that comes to mind, Herbie.

WAITKUS

Are you still here? I thought I told you to stay clear over to the other side of the room.

BLODGETT

Well, I just had one quick final question that came to mind, Herbie. How is your group able to get that big band sound into a song like "Holiday for Strings" when all you have is a piano player and a drummer and yourself on the oboe?

WAITKUS

It's not an oboe. It's a bassoon. And in addition to that—mind your own business.

BLODGETT

Well, I didn't mean to pry. But it just occurs to me that you began this medley with a number featuring a lot of saxophones. And then you went into one requiring a big brass section. And now you've done "Holiday for Strings." But all you have up here is a pianist and a drummer and yourself on the oboe.

WAITKUS

It's not an oboe. It's a bassoon.

BLODGETT

Is that the only comment you have to make?

WAITKUS *(Getting defensive)*

Well, what else do you want me to say?

BLODGETT

Well, I thought you might explain how you're able to play three completely different styles of music when all you have in your group is a piano and a drum and that thing you're playing.

WAITKUS

I suppose you won't leave me alone until I give you an answer.

BLODGETT

Probably not.

WAITKUS *(Breaking down)*

Well, the truth is that there's a fourth member in my group. He's the one who puts on old records that go out over the P.A. system while the rest of us pretend we're playing. I'm not proud of that fact. But there's not much else we can do. A piano and a drum and a bassoon sound awful playing dance music.

BLODGETT

Yes. I can see how they would. So just dry your tears and try not to feel so ashamed. Anyone in your position might have been forced to do the same thing.

WAITKUS *(Tearfully)*

Thanks. That's nice of you to say. Now, as I raise my baton—here's a number dedicated just to you and your listeners.

BLODGETT

Fine. And once again, here's Herbie Waitkus and his orchestra.

(A Xavier Cugat number)

BLODGETT

Now, our time is up. So amid the strains of another toe-tapping number played in the Herbie Waitkus style, this is Buddy Blodgett bidding you a fond farewell—and returning you to our New York studios.

(A few more beats of music, then sharp cutoff)

Special Report

BOB

We now take you live to London. An American TV reporter has pitched camp on the lawn of Buckingham Palace and vows to stay until Prince Charles comes out and grants him an exclusive interview. This determined newsman is Rex Grippner of WVTV-TV in Baraboo, Wisconsin . . .

GRIPPNER

Now hold it a second! *(Shouting through bullhorn)*: I know you're in there, Charlie! And the longer you hold out, the longer I'm gonna be.

BOB

Was that the Prince of Wales you were shouting at?

GRIPPNER

Yeah. I thought I saw him peeking out through the drapes. But it may have been just a liveried footman or some other flunky.

BOB

You feel you have the right to yell threats at the Prince that way?

GRIPPNER

Look: He's kept me waiting five days for an interview. And I've got better things to do. There's a big cattle show in Belgium this week for one thing.

BOB

Put it this way. Why should the Crown Prince grant an exclusive interview to a reporter from Baraboo, Wisconsin?

GRIPPNER

Because he's big news. It's not just a local story when a prince gets married and goes on his honeymoon. People back home want to hear all the spicy details, too.

BOB

And Prince Charles should come out here on the castle lawn and tell you all the intimate plans for his marriage and honeymoon?

GRIPPNER

If he didn't want the publicity that goes with the job, he never should have taken up princing! (Picks up bullhorn and shouts) I'm warning you, Chuck! I can wait this thing out as long as you can!

BOB

Was he peeking again?

GRIPPNER

No. I thought I saw him through that next window, stepping into the shower. But I guess it was just some woman.

BOB

Well, Mr. Grippner, I'm appalled that you don't think the royal family has any right to privacy.

GRIPPNER

I never said that. I'm not even sure that woman in the shower is a member of the royal family.

BOB

I'm talking about Prince Charles's marriage. He doesn't have to come out here and discuss it with you just because you're a news reporter.

GRIPPNER

Listen, Mac. That young fella visited the White House a couple of weeks ago. And it was the farmers in Baraboo, Wisconsin, who donated a thirty-four-pound turkey for his formal banquet. He owes us one for that!

BOB

Well, that may seem like a valid point but . . .

GRIPPNER *(On bullhorn)*

I'm giving you just one more day to come out, Chuckie Baby. Then I'm coming in after you.

BOB

Prince Charles held a news conference the day he announced his engagement. Why didn't you ask him your questions then?

GRIPPNER

I couldn't be here that day. I was too busy—back in the States—camping in the yard of one of the hostages from Iran. And he wouldn't come out and talk to me, either!

BOB

Well at least your luck is consistent! Now, from Buckingham Palace . . . it's back to our main studio.

GRIPPNER *(On bullhorn)*

Okay, Charlie . . . this is it!

The Komodo Dragon Expert

RAY

Have you noticed the "in vogue" words—words that you seem to hear more and more every day? Words like "pejorative" . . . "charisma" . . . and "dichotomy." Susskindisms, we call them. (And I use that in the pejorative sense.) And—"expertise." You seem to hear that every day more and more. Expertise implies that you're listening, I guess, to the words of an expert, and that's one thing we have plenty of here . . . experts. We're fortunate to have with us, now, the world renowned Komodo dragon authority from Upper Montclair, New Jersey. His name is Doctor Daryll Dexter. Doctor, would you tell everybody all about the Komodo dragon, please?

DEXTER

The Komodo dragon is the world's largest living lizard. It's a ferocious carnivore. It's found on the steep-sloped island of Komodo in the lesser Sunda Chain of the Indonesian Archipelago and the nearby islands of Rinja, Padar, and Flores.

RAY

Where do they come from?

DEXTER

Your Komodo dragon, the world's largest living lizard, is found . . . in the lesser Sunda Chain of the Indonesian Archipelago . . . and the nearby islands of Rinja, Padar, and Flores. We have two in this country at the National Zoo in Washington . . . which were given to us by the late former Premier of Indonesia . . . Sukarno . . . some years ago.

RAY

I believe I read somewhere . . . that a foreign potentate gave America some Komodo dragons. Is that true?

DEXTER

Yes . . . the former Premier of Indonesia, Sukarno, gifted this country with two Komodo dragons—world's largest living lizards . . . some years back . . . and they're now residing at the National Zoo in Washington.

RAY

Well, now, if we wanted to take the children to see a Komodo dragon . . . where would we take the children to see a Komodo dragon?

DEXTER

If you were in the vicinity of our nation's capital, Washington, D.C. . . . you would take the kiddos to the National Zoo, and there you would see two Komodo dragons . . . the world's largest living lizard. There is a stuffed Komodo dragon in the lobby of the Royal Hotel in Katmandu, Nepal.

RAY

Er—they're of the lizard family?

DEXTER

Yes. They are the world's largest living lizard and a ferocious carnivore. One swipe of the Komodo dragon's tail can render an enemy senseless.

RAY

Doctor . . . I believe we've just about exhausted the subject. I want to thank you for coming here from Upper Montclair. I know it was a great hardship for you to get here today. Do you have a ride home?

DEXTER

No, I don't.

RAY

Well, maybe somebody from the audience will give you a ride home after the show. I know we all know a great deal more now about the Komodo dragon than we did a few moments ago.

Editorial: The Leash Law

BOB

Now, in the interest of good broadcasting, we have a reply to a recent Bob and Ray editorial, in which we expressed the view that the New York City law requiring leashes for dogs should be broadened to include cats, hamsters, and other pets. Here now to speak in response is Mr. Victor J. Bodenhamer of the National Society of Friends of the Four-Legged. Go right ahead, Mr. Bodenhamer.

BODENHAMER

Well, I certainly intend to. The attitude shown by you two birds toward my presence here today has been a humiliating experience.

BOB

Well, I'm sorry you feel that way, sir. Actually, we were just discussing our general reaction toward listeners who come here to present editorial rebuttals. And of course, nothing we said was meant as a personal reflection on you.

BODENHAMER

What are you talking about? Your pal, Fatso, called me a little shrimp. That's about as personal as you can get. And I don't like it one bit.

BOB

Well, I can understand that. But by the same token, you just referred to Ray as Fatso. And he has a legion of friends who only think of him as heavyset.

BODENHAMER

Yeah? Well, I've got a legion of friends who only think of me as being petite or diminutive—but never as a little shrimp.

BOB

Well, I'm sure . . .

BODENHAMER

Excuse me. But if you'd allow me to finish making my point here— I'm only five-feet-two. But I'm very well proportioned, so that my small stature isn't even noticed unless I'm standing next to a normal person.

BOB

Well, I hope you're not saying that you think of yourself as being abnormal just because of your diminutive stature.

BODENHAMER

No. Not at all. That was just a Freudian slip. You see, I admit that I took quite a pushing around as a child because I was small. But now that I'm an adult, I have a legion of friends—as I mentioned a moment ago. Of course, you may not believe that.

BOB

Oh, yes. I believe it. You seem like a decent enough person to me.

BODENHAMER

Thank you. That's the first nice thing anybody's said to me since I got here.

BOB

Well, I'm sorry if the members of our staff have shown any hosility toward you, Mr. Bodenhamer. I guess they just act a little cold when anybody shows up to challenge one of our editorials.

BODENHAMER

Really? I thought they were being snippy toward me just because I'm
short.

BOB

No—not at all.

BODENHAMER

Well, a lot of people do, you know. They figure that a little twerp like
me can't stand up to normal people. So they really let me have it—
just to make themselves feel big and important.

BOB

Well, I can assure you, Mr. Bodenhamer, that our staff shows the same
rotten attitude toward every guest who comes here to deliver an editorial reply. And we've had several who were well over six feet tall.

BODENHAMER

No kidding! Gee, you've really made me feel a lot better by saying that.
I guess I was just being overly sensitive about my size.

BOB

Well, it's only natural that you would be. As you said, you took quite a
pummeling as a child because you were short. And the effects of an
experience like that can last a lifetime.

BODENHAMER

That's very true. But not many normal-size people have the human
compassion to understand that. I've really enjoyed meeting you, and
having this little conversation.

BOB

Well, thank you. Now is there anything . . .

BODENHAMER

If you're ever out in East Islip, you must stop in for dinner. Just give me a call from the station and I'll come over and pick you up.

BOB

Well, that's very kind of you, sir. But now, what about your editorial rebuttal?

BODENHAMER

Well, I don't believe there's anything else I need to add. So thanks for everything. You've been a real peach. Good-bye.
(Sound: Footsteps and door slam)

BOB

You have been listening to a reply to a recent Bob and Ray editorial on the subject of broadening New York's present leash law for dogs. Speaking was Mr. Victor L. Bodenhamer, the little shrimp who represents the National Society of Friends of the Four-Legged. Printed copies of this editorial rebuttal will not be available to the public—so please don't write in asking for one. Thank you.

RAY

Yes. Especially for not writing in—thank you!

Tippy, the Wonder Dog

BOB

And now Mushies—the great new cereal that gets soggy even without milk or cream—brings you another exciting story of adventure starring Tippy, the Wonder Dog.

(Sound: Dog bark)

BOB

As we look in on the isolated cabin of Grandpa Witherspoon today, we find that a herd of cattle has broken out of a nearby corral, and is stampeding through the valley. Gramps has crawled underneath his cot in a desperate effort to escape the approaching stampede, as little Jasper stands in the front window—gazing out at the quiet lull before the storm. Suddenly, the boy turns and speaks . . .

JASPER

No cows out there now, Gramps. Do you think maybe it's just the quiet lull before the storm?

GRANDPA

Consarn it all! You bet your boots it's just the quiet lull before the storm. That's why I sent that fool dog of yours out for some barbed wire to string around our property before the stampede gets here. Those critters aren't cows like you seem to think, boy. They're full-grown steers.

JASPER

Okay. Sorry for the incorrect terminology, Gramps. But aside from that, you don't need to worry about a thing. Tippy'll be here with your barbed wire momentarily. He's the dependablest, smartest dog in the whole world.

GRANDPA

Well, consarn it all—then where is he? I sent him to the store for fencing material when I heard the stampede was headed this way early Saturday morning.

JASPER

Well, there are a lot of different kinds of barbed wire to choose from. And it always takes Tippy a while to select his purchase when it involves comparison shopping. But I'm sure he'll be along soon. Tippy's the finest, smartest . . . Hark! I think I see him out there now, Gramps— headed home lickety-split to save us from getting trampled.
(*Sound: Door open. Hoof beats and mooing of cattle stampede*)

JASPER

Here, Tippy, Tippy, Tippy.
(*Sound: Door shut. Stampede noise out*)

GRANDPA

Consarn it all. Give me that barbed wire quick. I can hear those cattle stampeding right outside the door.

JASPER

I think it was just your vivid imagination, Gramps. I didn't hear anything. Besides, that wasn't Tippy out there after all. It was just that

Airedale of the Padgetts. He was headed home with a case of electric cattle prods—batteries included.

GRANDPA

Consarn it all. Every other dog in the neighborhood is helping his master get ready for the stampede. But that fool Tippy probably just got a safe distance away, and then crawled up to take a nap.

JASPER

Aw, Gramps, you always turn your venom on Tippy when you get scared of being crushed by cattle. But he won't let you down. He's the dandiest, smartest . . . Wait! I see him out there now.
> (Sound: Door open. Hoofbeats and mooing of cattle stampede)

JASPER

Here, Tippy, Tippy, Tippy.
> (Sound: Door shut. Stampede noise out)

GRANDPA

Consarn it all! Where's my barbed wire? Those critters sounded like they were ready to come right through the door.

JASPER

I didn't hear a thing. In addition to which—I might add—that wasn't Tippy out there. It was just that puppy that hangs around the Robinson place. He was headed up that way with a carton of Halloween noise-makers. I guess they're used to scare cattle away.

GRANDPA

Consarn it all! That pup's no bigger than a minute. But he can still be sent out on errands I'd never trust to that fool Tippy.

JASPER

Aw gee, Gramps. I don't know why you always lash out at Tippy as a means of releasing your pent-up anxiety. He's the peachiest, smartest . . . Wait! I see him out there for sure now—loping up the path to save us again.
> (Sound: Door open. Hoofbeats and mooing of cattle stampede)

JASPER

Come on in, Tippy. That's my swell old dog.
(Sound: Door slam. Stampede noise out)

JASPER

I think I'm beginning to hear cows out there, too, Gramps.

GRANDPA

Consarn it all! They're not cows. They're steers. But never mind that. Just give me the barbed wire. Maybe I can still string it around the porch to keep us safe.

JASPER

Sorry, Gramps. But it looks as if the only items Tippy picked up at the store were this baseball bat and outdoor barbecue.

GRANDPA

Consarn it all! I'm going to make that fool dog wish he'd never been born.

JASPER

No! Wait, Gramps! Don't you see the clever thing Tippy has done on our behalf? He's figuring how we can profit from the cattle stampede by hitting one of those cows over the head with a baseball bat and then cooking the steaks on this outdoor barbecue. Boy, oh boy! Didn't I tell you, Gramps? Tippy's the brilliantest, smartest dog in the whole wide world.
(Sound: Dog bark)
(Theme: Establish and under for)

BOB

Today's thrilling story has been brought to you by Mushies, the great new cereal that gets soggy even without milk or cream. Join us soon for more spectacular adventure starring . . . Tippy, the Wonder Dog.

(Theme up briefly and then out)

Public Service Announcement: Elephant Keepers

BOB

We're happy to devote the next few seconds to an important public service announcement.

RAY

It's a message from the elephant keepers at the Bronx Zoo here in New York, and we're happy to cooperate. It's been brought to the attention of these keepers that certain citizens have been exploiting their elephants.

BOB

You know, these elephants are supported at the zoo for the edification of the taxpayers of New York City—as well as guests from out of town.

RAY

And the officials of the Zoological Society take a dim view of certain promotion-minded characters who have been painting advertising slogans on these elephants. For example: "Subscribe to the Casserly Memory Course and remember like me!"

BOB

Or "Let the Keen Express Company handle your trunks!"

RAY

These mercenary efforts are distasteful to all of us, and we ask your cooperation in helping stamp out the practice!

Martin LeSoeur, Raconteur

BOB

Now I'd like you to meet an old friend and a real joy as a guest, an author, traveler, a lecturer, adventurer . . . a bon vivant . . . raconteur . . . gourmet . . . gourmand . . . roué . . . and best of all a great storyteller. We all know him by his dapper little trademark, a pencil-thin moustache. Would you welcome, please, Mr. Martin LeSoeur.
(Noticing half of the moustache is missing)

BOB

Will you tell us how it happened, Martin?

LESOEUR

You mean my dapper little trademark?

BOB

Yes.

LESOEUR

Well, I just wasn't thinking when I shaved this morning . . . and half the trademark went on the floor.

BOB

I might add that Martin has agreed very generously to go through with this performance. But he has canceled all other engagements till it grows back. We're very grateful to him.

LESOEUR

My doctor tells me it will grow back in about three or four weeks.

BOB

Martin, everyone here is waiting, of course, for some of those stories that you're famous for, and only you can tell, and which we all remember and love. Could we have one of them now?

LESOEUR

Sure, Bob. As you know, when I first started in this business I was a cub reporter for the old *St. Paul Ledger, Dispatch, Eagle Tribune, Courier Citizen, Beacon Journal, Plain Dealer, Deseret News and Daily Item.*

BOB

That was a famous merger, wasn't it?

LESOEUR

Yes.

BOB

I remember reading about that when I was at Yale.

LESOEUR

I was in the city room one day and I heard the phone ring. I heard the editor talking . . . Seems that there was a man hanging from a ledge on the fifteenth floor of the Vaseline Building on Sixteenth and Walnut. So I said to the editor, can I go over there and cover that story.

BOB

That would be a big break for you as a newspaperman.

LESOEUR

Oh, I don't know. So he says, sure . . . take public transportation and go on over there.

BOB

What was that?

LESOEUR

Trolley car. So I get over there about twenty minutes later and he's still hanging there. There's a crowd of people, policemen, firemen with their nets. So I asked if anybody had tried to use any humor on this fella. Tell him a few jokes, get his mind off his problem, talk him in.

BOB

Were you known at that time for having a sense of humor?

LESOEUR

Not particularly. So I asked if they would mind if I tried. So they said go right ahead. So I go over to the building and there was no elevator.

BOB

You mean you had to climb fifteen flights?

LESOEUR

Fifteen floors. I get up there and there's a policeman standing there outside the door. So I says I've been authorized to go in and talk to this man.

BOB

Right.

LESOEUR

So he says go ahead. So I go in and I go over to the window and . . . I said . . .

(LeSoeur points to the window. Long pause)

BOB

What did you say to him?

(More waiting)

BOB

Martin, maybe that will come back to you later in the program. I remember when you were here not too long ago, you told us a great story about fishing off the Grand Banks.

LESOEUR

Oh, my, yes. I was doing a fifteen-hundred-word article for a magazine on fishing in the North Atlantic.

BOB

That is a cold, rigorous, tough life, isn't it?

LESOEUR

It's not for me. It was in the middle of November, we were on a fishing smack, the *Rita B.*, up off the Grand Banks of Nova Scotia. And they're pulling in all this cod, mackerel, haddock, and halibut, and everything . . . and I look over here to the starboard and I see a submarine surface with a foreign insignia on it.

BOB

Was this wartime?

LESOEUR

No, no. So I turned to the captain . . . and "Captain," I said . . .
    (*LeSoeur points to his left and again can't remember the finish to the story. He looks to his right and points as if to remember the first story . . . then back to the captain. Bob glances at his watch. Long pause*)

BOB

Well, we do have to move along. Do you have one story that you know the ending to?
    (*LeSoeur reaches inside his coat and pulls out a piece of paper*)

LESOEUR

I wrote one down so I wouldn't forget it.

BOB

Good.

LESOEUR

It goes like this: "Well, that's all right, but this is Tuesday."
(Laughs uncontrollably)
"This is Tuesday!"

BOB

Okay! Good! Now—What is the story that leads up to that ending?
(LeSoeur looks blank. Fiddles with the paper. Long pause)

BOB

Martin, I hope the next time we invite you on our show, your memory and your moustache will both be improved. Thanks anyway . . . Martin LeSoeur . . .

Monongahela Metal Foundry #2

RAY

Say, here's a timely reminder from your friends at the Monongahela Metal Foundry. There's no one time of the year when there's not a chance of friends or relatives dropping in at your house. Having unexpected guests see your dull steel ingots is an embarrassing prospect for everyone.

BOB

But, it's a fear you can banish forever—once you've visited your Monongahela Foundry showroom and stocked up on those extra shiny steel ingots you'll be proud to display. Don't let unexpected company think you're a person with corroded ingots. See your local Monongahela sales agent today.

Bob and Ray Was There: The Invention of the Safety Pin

RAY

And now, through the courtesy of the Ashenfelter Whip Socket Company, we take you back to . . .

BOB *(Echo chamber)*

April ninth, 1872! Harlan Spivey, Junior, invents the safety pin. Bob and Ray was there.

(Sound: door shut)

MOM

My stars, Junior. What have you been doing down in that basement workshop of yours? It seems as though you've been there for hours.

SPIVEY

Actually, it's been longer than that, Mother. This is the first time I've come up from the basement in eight months. I was determined to stay

down there until I thought of a successful invention. Then I can make
enough money to get an apartment of my own.

MOM

An apartment of your own? My word, Junior. I don't know what gets
into young people's heads these days. Why would you want to run
away from home?

SPIVEY

Well, I don't look upon it as running away from home, Mother. I'm
forty-three years old. I've just never been financially able to make it on
my own before now. But look what I've invented to change all that.

MOM

Well, it's a cute little thing. But what in the world does it do? It just
looks like an oval-shaped piece of metal wire with a spring at one end.

SPIVEY

Well, it only looks that way when it's closed, Mother. But see what
happens when I press against the side of the metal wire. The clasp
opens and a pointy end pops out over here.

MOM

Yes. I see it does. Un-huh . . . You know, Junior—it's foolish things
like this you do that have made me keep you here at home all these
years. I can't imagine who'd want a piece of bent wire that has one
pointy end fitting inside a metal clasp.

SPIVEY

Aw, for Pete's sake, Mother. I don't know why you have to belittle
everything I invent. It's no wonder I've never built up enough self-
confidence to leave home and get my own apartment.

MOM

Well, Junior, we went through all this before when you invented the
telephone and the electric light bulb. You're just lucky I was here to
make you see that nobody would want those things before you went
out and made a fool of yourself. Now you've come up with another
invention that's just as silly.

SPIVEY

But this isn't silly, Mother. Let me show you. See how you can run the pointy end through these pieces of paper—just as simple as an ordinary straight pin. But then after you've got all your papers together—you can put the pointy end back inside the clasp so you won't stick yourself with it.

MOM

Well, I guess that would hold papers together. But it seems like an awfully complicated device for doing it—just to keep from sticking yourself with a pin point. What do you call this gadget, anyway?

SPIVEY

I think I'll call it a paper clip, Mother. And I'm convinced that the world is ready for it.

MOM

Well, I don't know what to say, Junior. It just seems as though you ought to be able to make something out of metal to hold papers together that would be cheaper to manufacture.

SPIVEY

Aw, Mother. You're just determined to find fault with every invention I think of. All you care about is keeping me here at home. There couldn't be a better gadget than this to hold papers together—and you know it.

MOM

Well, throwing a tantrum about it isn't going to do you any good. You'd be better off trying to think of some way to improve this paper clip of yours. That pointy end's still dangerous. And besides—if you wanted to take one paper out of the middle of the stack—you'd have to unpin the whole thing and then pin them all back together again.

SPIVEY (*Getting hysterical*)

I don't want to hear any more of your criticism. This is a real good invention—but you just won't admit it. Show me a better way to hold papers together if you're so smart.

MOM

Well, I suppose you could just twist an ordinary piece of wire around until you made some kind of clamp out of it. Then you wouldn't need a pointy end and a clasp that opens and closes and all that.

SPIVEY

No! It wouldn't work. And you're a mean old woman to say it would.

MOM

Now, Junior. If you want to hold your papers together with one of those things—Mother won't object.

SPIVEY

No! I don't want to anymore. You've spoiled it all now. And I'm going downstairs and break the mold for this gadget into a million, billion pieces.

(Sound: Footsteps and door slam)

RAY

And so Harlan Spivey, Junior—in a fit of rage—destroyed his machinery for making the first workable safety pin. However, his efforts did inspire his mother to become rich and famous through her invention of the first workable paper clip. And what sort of day was it? A day like all days that alter and illuminate our times. The date?

BOB *(Echo chamber)*

April ninth, 1872. Harlan Spivey, Junior, invents the safety pin. Bob and Ray was there.

The Do-It-Yourselfer

RAY

Now it's time once again to pick up some valuable tips for you home handymen as we pay another of our regular visits to the basement workshop of Fred Falvy, the do-it-yourselfer. And Fred—I'm glad I found you at home today. When I saw all those rolled-up newspapers out in your front yard, I was afraid you might be away on vacation.

FALVY

Oh, no, Ray. I rolled up all those papers and scattered them around the yard about a week ago. It's part of a do-it-yourself project I'm involved in.

RAY

Well, I can't imagine what it is, Fred—unless it has something to do with all the burglars you'll attract by creating the impression that you're away from home.

FALVY

No. I admit that having all those rolled-up papers in the yard does
attract a few prowlers who think the place is deserted. But what little
they steal is more than offset by the money I save from leaving papers
out there until they get good and soggy.

RAY

You just leave them out there in the rain and snow until that happens,
eh?

FALVY

Oh, yes. You see, the idea is to let nature convert the newspapers back
into wood pulp. And then you can burn them in the fireplace just like
logs. Only the cost is much less, of course.

RAY

Well, it certainly sounds like another wonderful example of better living
by doing it yourself, Fred. But how long does it take for the natural
elements to turn newspapers back into wood pulp?

FALVY

I'm really not sure, Ray. I read in a book where it would take about
two hundred thousand years for paper to become converted into coal.
But I'm certain that changing it into wood pulp wouldn't take near
that long.

RAY

Well, then I suppose it could even happen within our lifetime. And
it'll be a real money saver if it does. Now, I know that all our beloved
friends of the radio audience are anxious to hear about the do-it-
yourself project that you've chosen to describe today.

FALVY

Today, I've chosen a real money-saving project to describe for our
beloved friends of the radio audience, Ray. I'm sure most of us are
aware that handmade lampshades have gone up in price faster than
the general cost of living.

RAY

No. I wasn't aware of that, Fred.

FALVY

Well, most people are aware of it, Ray. However, it's not generally known that do-it-yourselfers can make lovely lamp shades right in the basement workshop—just using some inexpensive equipment and a few simple tools.

RAY

Well, I noticed that you have some blue paper stacked up here on the workbench. Is that what you're using for your lampshade project?

FALVY

Yes. This paper is good, sturdy twenty-pound bond, Ray. It comes cut into eight-and-a-half-by-eleven sheets as a rule. And the color of these particular sheets is blue.

RAY

Yes. I didn't know about the size and weight. But I noticed it was blue.

FALVY

Well, you can get it in almost any color you want, Ray. It's just ordinary mimeograph stock. And the paper mill here in the neighborhood where I bought these sheets also had it in white and pink and yellow. I don't think they make mimeograph paper in black. But you probably wouldn't want to use black for a lampshade anyway.

RAY

No. I imagine black paper would absorb too much light. So what do you do after you've selected the color for your lampshade? Do you make some kind of wire frame to stretch the paper across?

FALVY

Oh, no. You don't have to get into all that. You just roll a sheet of paper into sort of a cone shape—taking care to leave the small end large enough to fit around a bulb socket. And then you staple the edges of your paper together using an ordinary office stapler filled with Number Five wire staples. Here. I'll show you how that's done.

(Sound: Stapling machine)

RAY

Fred is stapling along the edge of his rolled-up sheet of paper. And that certainly is making it stay in the conical shape you want, Fred. But I don't quite know what you're going to do with it now.

FALVY

Well, the rest is actually quite easy, Ray. I just unscrew this bulb hanging down from the ceiling here. Then I put my blue paper shade around the socket—like this. And then as I screw the bulb back in, that holds my cone-shaped piece of paper where I want it. That's why I rolled the paper into a cone to make the shade in the first place—so the bulb would hold it in place.

RAY

I see. Well, of course, this piece of blue paper you've stapled together makes a fine shade for a naked bulb hanging down from the ceiling. But there aren't many fixtures like that around any more. What if you want a shade for a regular lamp?

FALVY

Oh, well, you can buy those at any lampshade store, Ray. It's the ones for these old-time ceiling fixtures that are hard to locate. I went to six or seven stores and couldn't find a one.

RAY

Well, then, you can save time as well as money by making your own—if you happen to be one of those rare individuals with an old-time ceiling fixture. So we could certainly say that this is just one more prime example of how to live better by doing it yourself. And we've been privileged to hear all about it directly from the basement workshop of Fred Falvy, the do-it-yourselfer.

Emergency Ward

RAY
And now the United States Mint . . . one of the nation's leading producers of fine new money . . . presents another dramatic story from the files of *Emergency Ward*.

                    (Organ: Dramatic theme)

SNUTTON

Greetings and welcome. I am Doctor Gerhard Snutton—handsome young physician who has not yet established a practice of his own. Instead, I work in the emergency ward of a big city hospital. The emergency ward is a place where the saga of human misery unfolds twenty-four hours a day. Take the other evening, for example. I was utilizing a spare moment to engage in some medical research when my associate, Nurse Rudehouse, turned to me and said . . .

RUDEHOUSE

Why are you standing on top of the desk waving that flyswatter around, Doctor?

SNUTTON

I'm proving that a long-held scientific theory of mine is correct, Nurse Rudehouse. The mere sight of a flyswatter is enough to scare flies away. That means they have enough mentality to learn what can hurt them.

RUDEHOUSE

Well, I don't see how you can prove a thing like that in a hospital, Doctor. We're careful not to let any flies in here.

SNUTTON

That's what I just finished telling you, Nurse Rudehouse. There aren't any flies in here. And that's because they all saw me standing on this desk waving my flyswatter around.

(Door opens. Loud metallic twang. Door closes)

MAN

Pardon me. Is this the emergency ward of a big city hospital?

SNUTTON

Yes. And I am Doctor Gerhard Snutton, handsome young physician who has not yet established a practice of his own. I might also mention that the salad fork you have sticking out your ear just scraped against our woodwork as you came through the doorway.

MAN

Yeah. I'm sorry about that. I tried not to damage your paint. But this all ties in with my medical emergency. You see, my wife tried out a new recipe on me tonight. And I didn't like it. So she got mad and stuck this salad fork in my ear.

SNUTTON

I'll have to prepare you for X-rays. It could be a punctured ear drum.

MAN

No. I think it was tomato aspic with little pieces of pineapple in it. But you don't have to take X-rays, Doc. I didn't swallow any of it.

SNUTTON

I mean X-rays of your ear to see if there's been damage, dumbbell.

RUDEHOUSE

Well, Doctor—I don't think his ear drum could be punctured. He seems to hear you all right.

SNUTTON

That's because I'm a physician, and he knows he'd better pay attention when I'm speaking to him, Nurse Rudehouse.

RUDEHOUSE

Well, I don't see how that could enter into it.

SNUTTON

I don't expect you to understand technical relationships like that. After all, you never spent a day of your life in medical school.

MAN

Excuse me. But if you people are planning to have a fight, I think I'll go get a drink of water.

SNUTTON

Very well. Just don't get any water in your ear. That could spoil the X-ray pictures.

MAN

Okay. I'll be careful. And I'll only be gone a minute.
                    (Loud metallic twang)

MAN

Sorry.

SNUTTON

Clumsy oaf! Now, Nurse Rudehouse, I want you to call the X-ray department and make a reservation with the photographer on duty.

RUDEHOUSE

I think they call them X-ray technicians, Doctor—not photographers.

SNUTTON

Well, whoever they are—I'd prefer that young redhead who just joined the staff, if she's on duty this evening.

MAN

Hey, Doc—Look! When I bent over the water fountain—I must have tilted my head to one side—and the salad fork fell out.

SNUTTON

Well, that's only a natural reaction that you shouldn't be alarmed about. It's the law of gravity. I studied it in medical school.

MAN

Gee. It's really nice to have an educated man like you around to explain these things when they happen. But anyway, I seem to be cured. So what do I owe you, Doc?

SNUTTON

Well, the X-rays would have been seventy-five dollars. But since we never took those I guess a dollar and a half should take care of everything.

MAN

That seems about right—considering how serious my condition might have been. So here you are—and thanks for everything. Good-bye.
(Footsteps and door closes)

SNUTTON

Well, Nurse Rudehouse, you have just seen another hopeless victim walk out of here in radiant good health—thanks to the wonders of medical science. So just make a brief notation in your case book: Patient released—cured.

(Organ: Theme. Establish and under for)

RAY

Join us again soon when the United States Mint—one of the nation's leading producers of money—will bring you another dramatic story from the files of . . . *Emergency Ward.*

(Organ. Theme up briefly and then out)

The P's and Q's Minder

BOB

It's new ideas time . . . and here is Mr. Leonard P. Harkness to tell us just how he began what we feel is a most unusual business venture. Welcome to the show, sir.

HARKNESS

Thanks, very much, Bob, and hello to you folks in radio land.

BOB

Tell us just how you started this unusual business, will you?

HARKNESS

Well, it all started back several years ago. I went to my boss with a suggestion and he told me to mind my own P's and Q's. Fortunately, I saw the wisdom in that statement, and I've been minding my own P's and Q's ever since.

BOB

And now, I believe you've gone into the thing commercially?

HARKNESS

Yes. I'm now minding P's and Q's for other people who are too busy
to do it.

BOB

How many clients do you have?

HARKNESS

I have fifty people now for whom I am minding their P's and Q's.

BOB

Minding fifty people's P's and Q's! That's wonderful!

HARKNESS

Well, I don't know. Sometimes I get kind of sick of 'em. I'd like an R
to show up once in a while. You know what I mean?

BOB

I can imagine.

HARKNESS

Oh, P's and Q's aren't bad. You get used to them. But I'd give anything
to have a good old-fashioned T, or W, maybe, to mind.

BOB

Well, after all, in your business you *are* specializing.

HARKNESS

I have to specialize, yes, since it's just P's and Q's.

BOB

Can you tell us how you go about minding someone's P's and Q's?

HARKNESS

Well, I just go over to them and we sign a contract. From then on, I
mind their own P's and Q's. They don't have to watch out for them

any more. I don't want to say how I do it exactly. As it is now, I don't
have many competitors.

BOB

I understand. And competition could become keen.

HARKNESS

Yes. What I'm afraid of is that somebody may come out with minding
somebody's M and M's. And even L O P's . . . Like that.

BOB

Or B and B's.

HARKNESS

Exactly.

BOB

J and B's?

HARKNESS

Don't mind if I do.

BOB

Well, the idea has all sorts of possibilities, but for now as long as you
manage your own P's and Q's, you seem all set.

HARKNESS

I might mention that if anyone listening in would like to have their
own P's and Q's minded by me, I'd be tickled to death to do it.

BOB

Just address Bob and Ray, care of . . .

HARKNESS

I'll give the address! You just mind your own P's and Q's!

BOB

Sorry.

HARKNESS

Just sign this contract, and from now on you don't have to have another worry about a P and a Q. I'll mind 'em for you.

BOB

Thanks, Leonard P. Harkness for being our guest on our *New Ideas Show*.

Wally Ballou Visits a
Paper Clip Factory

RAY

We've been conducting a cross-country search for inflation fighters—industrialists who've been going all-out in their efforts at cutting costs, eliminating waste, and contributing to the economic health of our nation. This week, Wally Ballou visited the Great Lakes Paper Clip Factory in Napoleon, Ohio—and here's his report.

BALLOU

——ly Ballou at the Great Lakes Paper Clip Factory in the office of its president, Mr. Hudley Pierce. And I want to thank you, Hudley, for the warm welcome you've given me here.

PIERCE

It's quite all right, Wally—always glad to have guests.

BALLOU

I might say I was amazed to find such a big plant as yours here is devoted to the production of such a small item as the paper clip.

PIERCE

Well, actually, there are much larger paper clip factories than ours, Wally. We're really one of the "little fellows" in the industry. But I guess we have to fight the same battles as the big boys. Battles against inefficiency . . . waste . . .

BALLOU

Now, I've only been through that one building, but I imagine there are others. In the one I saw, I was surprised that there's no machinery in there at all!

PIERCE

No, we don't have any machinery. We just buy wire in long strips. Then, our workers cut the strips into shorter pieces and bend them into paper clips.

BALLOU

Well, if all of this work is done by hand, I imagine you have to get a pretty hefty price for your product.

PIERCE

No. Our clips are priced competitively. So far, I think we've managed to hold the line on inflation—and we expect to keep on doing that. Our clips retail at ten cents for a box of one hundred.

BALLOU

Wow!

PIERCE

And we sell them there at the factory for six cents a box. In gross lots.

BALLOU

Astounding figures. How many boxes can a plant the size of yours turn out in, say, a week?

PIERCE

Well, when we have all three shifts working, we can produce right around two hundred boxes a week. If we can sell them all, that means we take in twelve dollars.

BALLOU

And you can afford to operate a big plant like that when your weekly sales only mount to twelve dollars?

PIERCE

Yes. We have a very low wage structure. Here, again, we've been able to hold the line on costs. Our average worker makes about fourteen cents a week.

BALLOU

Well how in the world could anybody live on that?

PIERCE

We don't pry into the personal lives of our employees, Wally. But I understand that most of our people live in caves out at the edge of town. And they forage for food.

BALLOU

Apropos of that, I noticed on my visit to the plant that all of the fellows working there were dressed in rags. And they seemed to have strips of cloth tied around their feet!

PIERCE

Well you can't wear shoes when you make fourteen cents a week. That should be fairly obvious to anybody.

BALLOU

Probably explains why they seemed to be grumbling, too . . .

PIERCE

Possibly . . .

BALLOU

I just can't understand how you can get people to work for a salary like that!

PIERCE

Well, the union contract has quite a few loopholes in it. For example, it doesn't mention wages at all. But, it does have a clause that makes a worker subject to prosecution—and imprisonment—if he tries to quit!

BALLOU

I imagine the union will have that changed the first chance it gets.

PIERCE

Fortunately for the firm, it's a ninety-nine-year sweetheart contract. And it still has almost eighty-six years yet to run.

BALLOU

Well it's certainly been interesting to chat with you, Hudley, and we tip our hat to you in your valiant fight to cut costs and eliminate waste.

PIERCE

Thank you.

BALLOU

Now, this is peripatetic Wally Ballou returning it to Bob and Ray.

Einbinder Flypaper #2

RAY
Say . . . here's a home decorating tip from our kind subscriber, the makers of Einbinder Flypaper. Friends: Are you ashamed of hanging flypaper in your home that clashes with the color scheme of your other furnishings? If so, you should switch today to Einbinder, because genuine Einbinder Flypaper is offered only in a neutral tan shade that blends nicely with anything. Remember—gaudy striped or plaid flypaper may be all right for your downstairs rumpus room. But a conservative color is best for your living and dining areas. And the flypaper that's always in good taste is Einbinder—the brand you've gradually grown to trust over the course of three generations. Get some today.

Dining Out: The Far Rockaway House of Clam Chowder and Soda Crackers

RAY

And now . . . "Dining Out with Bob and Ray"—the informative feature that helps guide you to some of the lesser-known but truly outstanding gourmet restaurants around New York and the world. Bob, I believe you had an opportunity this week to visit one of those little specialty restaurants that our listeners are always searching for—but that seem so hard to find . . .

BOB

That's right, Ray. And I know everyone will want to make a note of this one. It's the Far Rockaway House of Clam Chowder and Soda Crackers.

RAY

Located, of course, in Far Rockaway.

BOB

No. Actually, it's located in Yonkers. However, the owner told me that his ancestors came from Far Rockaway several generations ago. So he's retained the sound of temple bells and the smell of exotic spices and all the other bits of atmosphere that we associate with Far Rockaway.

RAY

Well, it makes my pulse quicken just to hear about it. And I assume that the Far Rockaway House of Clam Chowder and Soda Crackers makes a specialty of serving clam chowder and soda crackers.

BOB

In fact, that's all they do serve, Ray. But like so many restaurants with a limited menu, the food is top quality. In fact, the owner told me that he has his supplies flown in fresh every day from Cedar Rapids, Iowa.

RAY

Really? That's very interesting. I didn't even know you could get clams from Cedar Rapids, Iowa.

BOB

Well, it's not the clams that come from there, Ray. It's the soda crackers. They're all stamped out by hand and baked in Cedar Rapids. But the old gentleman who makes them out there refused to spoil the taste by wrapping them in waxed paper. So, of course, they have to be flown to Yonkers every day so they won't get soggy.

RAY

Well, it sounds as if a lot of effort is put into the job of bringing crackers to your table as fresh as when they left the oven.

BOB

Yes. They come in a basket under a little crocheted blanket with the salted ones on one side and unsalted on the other.

RAY

Is that so? I haven't seen any unsalted soda crackers since I was a boy.

BOB

Well, I don't think I saw any even then. So it was a new taste treat for me. In fact, there was only one thing about the Far Rockaway House of Clam Chowder and Soda Crackers that wasn't really top drawer. That was the clam chowder. I think it came out of a can and was served at room temperature.

RAY

Well, I'm sure the delicious soda crackers more than made up for that.

BOB

Yes. I just skipped the chowder and filled up on crackers—which I'd suggest our listeners do, too. Now, I'm sure we'd all like to hear about the gourmet dining spot you visited this week, Ray.

RAY

Bob, the restaurant I'm recommending very strongly to all the folks who follow our "Dining Out" feature is Rudy's Show Time Grille. It's just a short, pleasant walk from the Kew Gardens Subway Station in a quaint little building that used to be a repair shop for vacuum cleaners.

BOB

Well, I'm sure I've read about Rudy's Show Time Grille. Isn't that the place with singing waiters to entertain you as you dine?

RAY

No. It has singing busboys. The waiters dance. And the maitre d' accompanies all the rest of them on the saxophone.

BOB

Well, it sounds charming. And is it a ballroom style of dancing where the waiters dance with each other?

RAY

No. It's more of a West Indian calypso type of music, Bob. I think the busboys are all from the Windward Islands or someplace down there. So calypso is about the only thing they're capable of singing.

BOB

I see. Well, I wouldn't think that would work out too well with a saxophone accompaniment by the maitre d'.

RAY

No. It doesn't. While I was there, the only song he played was "Everybody Loves My Marguerite." And that's not the same beat as calypso. But the waiters had formed a high-kicking chorus line. So that was a completely different tempo, too.

BOB

Un-huh. Well, I suppose that once you have two different types of music clashing, it doesn't hurt to add a third.

RAY

No. The whole show had just dissolved into a lot of good, clean fun by then. And several of the patrons joined in, too, because the food wasn't fit to eat.

BOB

Well, it sounds like a great place to spend an uninhibited evening. So I hope our listeners will all remember to jot down that name and location. It's Rudy's Show Time Grille near the Kew Gardens Subway Station. And now, Ray—I suppose that will do it until we both have time to search for more of those little known but truly fine gourmet restaurants around town.

RAY

Right you are. And, of course, we'll be reporting back on our discoveries very soon—when once again, it will be time to go "Dining Out with Bob and Ray."

The Big Scoop

(Theme: establish and under for)

BOB

Now we welcome you again to *The Big Scoop*—the program that pays tribute to the outstanding accomplishments of the nation's working newspapermen. And here at our news desk, prepared to tell you about this week's Big Scoop Award, is our Big Scoop Editor, Big Fred Scoop.

SCOOP

Thank you, Norman—and welcome to *The Big Scoop* This week's handsome award suitable for framing, together with a certified check for fifteen dollars, goes to Millard L. Peevy, the crime reporter for the *Kenosha, Wisconsin, Star-Tribune and Morning Throwaway*. It was only a little more than a year ago, on March fourteenth, 1981, that Millard Peevy's career took a sudden turn when he was called into the office of his managing editor.

(Newsroom noise)

EDITOR

Peevy—I've been wanting to speak to you personally because I plan to clean out some dead wood around the office. Naturally, you'll be the first to get the old heave-ho, unless you can explain what you've been doing the past few weeks. You haven't written a story for this paper since you covered the Eastern Star Rummage Sale on Lincoln's Birthday. Why have you been goofing off ever since then?

PEEVY

Actually, Chief, I've been working night and day on the story that could become my big scoop. Remember Big Daddy Gumbert, the guy who was sentenced to life in 1971 for hijacking a truckload of peach cobbler and killing the driver? Well, I'm convinced he didn't do it, Chief—and I'm out to prove that an innocent man is rotting in prison.

EDITOR

I can't believe you're serious, Peevy. I remember the Gumbert case well. The police found bits of stewed peaches on his shoes. Besides that, he dropped his driver's license and five credit cards in the cab of the hijacked truck when he abandoned it. His trial only lasted a half-hour before he was found guilty.

PEEVY

That was only because he signed a full confession, Chief. But I know now that he had to be shielding the real criminal. Too many things don't add up. And I intend to get to the bottom of this.

EDITOR

All right, Peevy. Follow up on your hunch if you want to. But if you're wrong and disgrace this newspaper, you're finished here at the *Kenosha, Wisconsin, Star-Tribune and Morning Throwaway*.

PEEVY

I understand, Chief. But as a working journalist, I'm honor bound to see that the guilty are punished and the innocent are set free. I'll put my career and my future on the line for that if I must.

(Stinger)

BOB

And so, Millard Peevy began the difficult job of searching for new evidence about a crime that had occurred ten years before. First, he sought out the medical man who headed the local police crime lab.

PEEVY

Doc—I'm convinced that someone ordered you to say that peach cobbler was found on the suspect's shoes—not to mention his fingerprints being found on the murder gun. Would you care to comment on why you committed perjury at the trial?

DOC

Why, you miserable wretch!
(Scuffle. Body falls)

BOB

Next, Peevy chatted with the retired police chief—who had been in charge of the force at the time of the Gumbert case.

PEEVY

Chief—it strikes me as quite a coincidence that you suddenly found you had enough money to retire only four years after Big Daddy Gumbert was put away for a murder he didn't commit. How about filling in the missing pieces for me on that?

COP

Why, you rotten little punk.
(Scuffle. Body falls)

BOB

Finally, Peevy went to the man who had been the prosecuting attorney in the Gumbert case—and had since gone on to become governor of the state.

PEEVY

Governor—I'm sure you know your political career will be finished once I break the story of your crooked, double-crossing background. So why not tell me all about it—and maybe I can go easy on you?

GOVERNOR

Why, you reprehensible pipsqueak.

(*Scuffle. Body falls*)

BOB

Armed with the facts, Millard Peevy returned to face his editor.

(*Newsroom noise*)

PEEVY

Sorry it took a few months longer than I expected, Chief. But you run into a lot of dead ends digging into a story like this. After all these years, the people involved were still determined to protect each other. And it takes a long time to chip away the alibis.

EDITOR

I understand, Peevy. But it was well worth the time if this paper can break the story that Big Daddy Gumbert is in prison for a crime he didn't commit.

PEEVY

Well, I'm afraid you'd better not run a story like that, Chief. This one I just wrote is safer. It's got all the documented facts in it to prove that Gumbert was guilty as sin. I don't know why I ever thought he might be innocent. But at least I can save you the trouble of firing me. Here's my concisely written letter of resignation. I've done my duty as a journalist, and now I'm finished.

(*Stinger*)

BOB

And so it was that Millard Peevy capped his long journalistic career with a fine job of investigative reporting that proved how our criminal courts had convicted a guilty man. Peevy now operates a shoeshine stand in the Kenosha bus depot. But at heart, he's still a newspaperman —and one whose story we've been privileged to tell here on . . . *The Big Scoop.*

(*Organ theme up*)

Alfred E. Nelson—Author

BOB

We're always impressed by the number of books about the history of our country which continually flow from the nation's publishers. It's apparently a very popular subject. And we've invited the author of a new history to be our guest. Welcome, please, Mr. Bonfiglio Rumplemyer.

NELSON

Hello, Bob.

BOB

I hope I got your name right. I can't quite make out the handwriting on this card you filled out, sir.

NELSON

Yeah, it's my writing again.

BOB

What is your name, then?

NELSON

Alfred E. Nelson.

BOB

And the title of the book you've just published?

NELSON

The History of the United States.

BOB

And I might say it's a heavy book . . . lots of pages . . .

NELSON

Yes, it has over eleven hundred pages and, of course, I'm just beginning to scratch the history of this country in it.

BOB

I've seen a review copy. And there seem to be a lot of questions raised by it.

NELSON

I might point out that it's profusely illustrated. I think you ought to mention that.

BOB

And it may help this little interview, Mr. Nelson. Here, just at random, is one of the pictures in your book:

BOB

You have Abraham Lincoln driving to his inauguration in an automobile!

NELSON

Yes. That is a definite error.

BOB

Did you check on that at all? I mean . . . it should have been fairly easy to . . .

NELSON

Oh, there are several glaring errors in the book that, unfortunately, I didn't catch. There was one referring to the Father of Our Country.

NELSON
WASHINGTON

BOB

You have "Nelson Washington" under his picture.

NELSON

Yes. I was just thinking of my last name, I guess. Because, of course, his first name was George. It's an honest mistake.

BOB

One of many. I seem to remember you listed the publisher of *Poor Richard's Almanac* as Benjamin French.

NELSON

Yes. It should have been Benjamin Franklin.

BOB

And look at this. "The First Capitol of the United States."

Bailey's Mistake, Maine:
First Capitol of the U.S.

BOB

Mr. Nelson, when did all these mistakes come to your attention?

NELSON

Well, a friend of mine brought them to my attention after the book was published. As soon as he got it he called me at home and started to point out several little errors that unfortunately got through. Like this one:

FDR Signs Social Security Act.

BOB

Another example of the sloppy work in your book!

NELSON

That was just carelessness on my part.

BOB

But did you check anything? Did you do any research on this book at all?

NELSON

Yes, I did considerable research, and, of course, I relied on my memory a great deal.

BOB

How far did you go in school, sir, if I may ask?

NELSON

Through the eighth grade.

BOB

And you wrote an eleven-hundred-page history with only . . .

NELSON

We had very intensive history courses!

BOB

Even so, an eighth grade education in American history is not enough to qualify a person, be he genius or not . . .

NELSON

That's what you say ! !

BOB

Well, this book proves it.

NELSON

I had all the facts. It was the names that were wrong. And the dates.
For instance, I had the Civil War happening in 1911 . . .

BOB

Yes, I know.

NELSON

Which was wrong. That, of course, I could have checked by asking
almost anybody. But here, again, when I sit down at the typewriter,
I just like to take off and go. Know what I mean?

BOB

Well, again, I must say it's a very sloppy job.

NELSON

Yes, it's a shabby piece of work. I'm one of the first to admit it.

BOB

And worst of all, it sells, I understand, for eighty-nine ninety-five—
which is a ridiculous price.

NELSON

It's leatherbound.

BOB

I don't care about the binding. That means nothing. It's what inside.

NELSON

It does mean something. It's leather, and the paper is glossy. It must
weigh ten or twelve pounds.

BOB

Well, all I can say is, I wouldn't want to show this to my children when
they ask me about history. I'm not going to look to this for a reference
work.

NELSON

Let me put it this way: I'll never appear on your show again, either!

BOB

That's perfectly all right with us, Mr. Nelson!

NELSON

Good-bye.

BOB

And sign out on your way out, please!

The Adventures of Charley Chew

(Organ: "Chinatown My Chinatown")

RAY

Now . . . the adventures of Charley Chew, famed Oriental sleuth, as he and his Number One Son attempt to solve . . . "The Case of the Mysterious Victim."

(Theme up and out)

INSPECTOR *(Fading in)*

. . . So that's the thing that has my men stumped about this case, Chew. The murder victim was found right here in the middle of the room wearing an army colonel's uniform. But there was no wallet or other identification on the body. So we don't know who he is.

CHEW

May I ask inspector one vital question?

NO. 1 SON

Good gravy, Pop! We've just barely arrived at the scene of a killing that has the police department stumped. And already your keen mind has thought of a vital question to ask.

CHEW

Number One Son like all-night gas station. Never shut up.

NO. 1 SON

Aw gee, Pop. I wish you didn't always have to be such a wet blanket. You know I get overly enthusiastic when I have a chance to help you work on a big murder case like this.

CHEW

Number One Son can best help illustrious father by holding breath until I beg you to stop—which may be late next week.

INSPECTOR

Chew, what was the vital question you wanted to ask?

CHEW

Wish to know whether other valuables also stolen from this room—or only wallet and identification of Colonel What's-His-Name.

INSPECTOR

Well, the people who live here aren't home. But from what we've observed—nothing else in the room has been touched. And that strikes me as strange because there's a diamond necklace right there on the table. Why would any crook rather steal the laundry tags out of a murder victim's clothing than a ten-thousand-dollar necklace?

CHEW

Inspector pose very interesting question. Now let us look at another question behind first question. Why would killer steal laundry tags unless he wished identity of victim to remain secret?

NO. 1 SON

Gee whiz, Pop! You don't keep a secret by stealing somebody's laundry tags. You keep a secret by making the other person cross his heart and hope to die. Of course—come to think of it—this guy died. So it all fits together.

CHEW

Number One Son like hermit who stay in house at top of hill. Never run down.

INSPECTOR

Chew—I can understand how that boy of yours would turn any father into a basket case. But just then, he almost made a valid point. Stealing laundry tags out of an army officer's uniform wouldn't keep his identity secret. There would be too many records on a military man at the Pentagon. But we've already checked the victim's dental work. And the army doesn't have a record of any colonel with two porcelain crowns on the left upper connected by bridgework.

CHEW

Charley Chew is most sad to discover how inspector has failed to learn anything of killer's M.O. One who is clever enough to remove laundry tags from uniform will also exchange victim's dental work for that of someone else. Hence, any wise detective will first seek aid of Pentagon in finding out who colonel lying at our feet could be.

NO. 1 SON

Holy cow, Pop! I see what you're driving at. We don't just give the Army this guy's dental records and ask who he is. Instead, we find out which army colonels are missing—and then figure out which one this victim might be.

CHEW

Charley Chew is pleased to note that blabbermouth son finally show intelligence inherited from father's side of family.

INSPECTOR

Well, I guess his comment might sound intelligent except for one thing, Chew. The Pentagon says there are no army colonels at all who are missing. So the victim isn't really an army colonel—and that leaves us facing a blank wall.

CHEW

Fear Inspector thinks wall is blank only because he is unable to decipher handwriting on it. Consider fact that victim is not truly a colonel. Yet, laundry tags have been removed from colonel's uniform worn by victim. Does this not then suggest that murderer himself was a colonel seeking to hide his own identity?

INSPECTOR

Yeah. It suggested that to me. But in addition to having *no* colonels missing—the army doesn't even have one within a hundred miles of here who's unaccounted for. So the victim and the killer have one thing in common. Neither one is an army colonel listed by the Pentagon.

CHEW

Ah, so. Very interesting.

NO. 1 SON

Hey, Pop! That's it! The inspector just said that the victim is not an army colonel listed by the Pentagon. But since he's wearing a colonel's uniform—then use the process of elimination, and you get the answer. He must be an army colonel who's *not* listed by the Pentagon. And there's only one of those, Pop. This man is the Unknown Soldier.

CHEW

Clever deduction by Number One Son proves wise saying of honorable ancestor: "Everybody must be somebody sometime."

NO. 1 SON

Gosh, Pop. If we had our honorable ancestors around now to give us their wise sayings—I'll bet we could make the police inspector look like an even bigger fool. *(chuckles)*

CHEW *(Joins chuckling)*
(Theme up and out)

Forbush Dinnerware Update

BOB

Friends: This is a pretty serious announcement we have coming up. If you were paying attention some time ago, you will recall that we offered two thousand four hundred and thirty-six sets of Forbush Dinnerware at the crazy price of a dollar ninety-eight.

RAY

Remember we said that our accountants told us we were crazy to have that many sets of genuine Forbush Dinnerware in our overstocked warehouse? And we said, "All right, we're crazy. So we'll unload them at the ridiculous, crazy figure of a dollar ninety-eight per set."

BOB

We said to you, our radio audience, that we had to unload these sets at that crazy price. We had to get them out of the warehouse no matter how much of a loss we took.

RAY

We emphasized the fact that we had to get them out of the warehouse. And that's what we meant. But we *did not* mean it the way one certain person took it, and we hope that person is listening right now!

BOB

Yesterday, when we made the statement that we had two thousand four hundred and thirty-six sets of genuine cracked Forbush Dinnerware in our warehouse, we *had* two thousand four hundred and thirty-six sets in our warehouse. But today we don't!

RAY

So . . . will the guy who backed a truck up to our warehouse last night and carried away two thousand four hundred and thirty-six sets of genuine cracked Forbush Dinnerware please return same at once?

BOB

We said we had to unload them. We said we had to get rid of them. We said we didn't care how much of a loss we took. But we didn't mean it that way!

RAY

Look, fellers: A joke is a joke, but let's not carry things too far! Just return those two thousand four hundred and thirty-six sets of genuine cracked Forbush Dinnerware, and we'll call it quits! It isn't the money —it's the principle of the thing.

BOB

That's right. And besides, we stand to lose in round figures $4,645.32.

RAY

So in the spirit of fair play, fellers, okay? And by the way, for those who are interested in a terrific bargain, whomever took those sets of genuine cracked Forbush Dinnerware from our warehouse last night must have tripped on the top step, because one full box was dropped.

BOB

If you want to get a box full of miscellaneous genuine *crushed* Forbush Dinnerware at a low, low, crazy price just write to *Debris,* care of Bob and Ray, New York!

Garish Summit—Episode #3

(*Theme: establish and under for*)

RAY

Welcome again to Garish Summit and its continuing story of intrigue among the socially prominent. There—in stately splendor far removed from the squalid village below—they fight their petty battles over power and money.

(*Theme up briefly and then fade for*)

RAY

As this week's action begins, young Rodney Murchfield is counting paper clips in his palatial office at the Murchfield Lead Mining Company. Suddenly, his evil brother Caldwell enters. Rodney speaks . . .

RODNEY

Five hundred and twenty-seven . . . five hundred and twenty-eight . . . five hundred and twenty-nine . . .

CALDWELL

I don't know whether you've heard about it yet, Rodney, but Mother just made me vice-president of the family business. Where should I put my golf clubs?

RODNEY

I really don't care. And I might add that the very idea of your being an officer of this firm fills me with disgust . . . five hundred and forty-eight . . . five hundred and forty-nine . . . five hundred and fifty . . .

CALDWELL

Well, I'm not too crazy about having you here either. But since you're president of the outfit, I'll try to make the best of it.

RODNEY

You're missing the point, Caldwell. My whole life has been dedicated to Murchfield Lead Mining. Lead is in my blood. Now, you've suddenly appeared as my long-lost brother—and I don't see that thirty years being long-lost qualifies you for an executive position.

(Door opens)

PAMELA

Excuse me. Would either of you care for some coffee?

RODNEY

Not now, Pamela. I'm in conference and can't be disturbed.

PAMELA

Yes, sir.

(Door closes)

RODNEY

Five hundred and eighty-six . . . five hundred and eighty-seven . . . five hundred and eighty-eight . . .

CALDWELL

Gee, I hope she comes back. I sure would have liked some coffee. Besides, I could tell she was giving me the big eye.

RODNEY

Caldwell, that young lady is in love with me, and I'm planning to leave my wife to marry her. It's scheduled for next Thursday, I believe. I have it here on my appointment pad somewhere.

CALDWELL

While you're looking for that, I'll outline my plans for changing our company's product line, now that I'm a big cheese here.

RODNEY

Don't talk nonsense. We can't change the product line. This is a lead mining company. Our only product is lead.
(Door opens)

PAMELA

Excuse me. If you're too busy for coffee, does that mean you want me to hold your calls, too?

RODNEY

Yes. By all means, Pamela—hold my calls.

PAMELA

Yes, sir. You haven't had any so far today. But if one comes in, I'll hold it.
(Door closes)

RODNEY

Frankly, Caldwell, I can't imagine why you'd suggest changing the firm's product line when this is only your first day on the job.

CALDWELL

Well, a business that only sells lead ingots just doesn't have much pizzazz. Besides, I saw a couple of our salesmen in the parking lot—and the poor guys couldn't even lift their sample cases.

RODNEY

Your compassion for the hired help is very touching, Caldwell. But if the men don't like it here, they can look for work in another state where we Murchfields don't control the economy.

(*Door opens*)

PAMELA

Excuse me—but since you're in conference, I thought this might be a good time for me to go to lunch.

RODNEY

Yes. Go to lunch, Pamela—by all means.

PAMELA

Thank you. I thought it might be a good idea to do that.

(*Door closes*)

RODNEY

It's hard to branch out from lead, Caldwell . . .

CALDWELL

Gee, I was hoping maybe she'd go to lunch with me. But you sure put the kibosh on that.

RODNEY

Pamela's my fiancée, Caldwell. I already told you that.

CALDWELL

Well, I plan to muscle in on you. But I guess that can wait.

RODNEY

Fine. Then let me complete my thought. We've made previous attempts to broaden the Murchfield product line with toy soldiers—fishing sinkers—all that sort of thing. In fact, we once adopted a new company motto: If it's heavy as lead, Murchfield makes it.

CALDWELL

Well, that's been your whole trouble. You can't see beyond lead. So I've taken steps to get us into the big money. Thanks to my efforts, there'll soon be a gambling casino operating on this very spot.

RODNEY

What in heaven's name are you talking about?

CALDWELL

Murchfield Lead has taken in a new partner, Rodney. I've settled an old personal debt by merging us with Big Otto from Detroit.
(Organ: musical sting)

RODNEY

I hope you're joking, Caldwell. Before I'd allow a thing like that to happen, I'd strangle you with my bare hands . . . six hundred and seventeen . . . six hundred and eighteen . . . six hundred and nineteen . . .
(Theme: establish and under for)

RAY

Can organized criminals fit in comfortably with the socially prominent Murchfields? And what about Pamela's mysterious failure to return from lunch? Perhaps we'll learn more next week when we hear Rodney say . . .

RODNEY

Now that I've signed the merger agreement, is it all right for me to take my feet out of the wet cement, Otto?

RAY

That's next week, when we resume our story of endless intrigue on *Garish Summit*.
(Theme up briefly and then out)

Monongahela Metal Foundry #3

B O B

Here's good news for you homemakers! You're well aware, I'm sure, that extra shiny steel ingots have been in short supply this season at your Monongahela Metal Foundry showroom. But now we're happy to say that supply has nearly caught up with the tremendous demand.

R A Y

You may still encounter a limit of three ingots to the customer in some scattered areas. But in most places, your Monongahela agent will be happy to sell you as many as you need to replace those old worn-out ingots you've been forced to use during the shortage. So, stock up today while there's a good selection.

Two Dog Trainers

BOB

Now—Bob and Ray are delighted to present two guests from the animal world! Our first guest signs in saying he is here with a troupe of performing French poodles. He signs in "Maitland W. Montmorency." Would you welcome him please? Maitland . . .

(Applause)

NORBIS

Actually my name is John W. Norbis. I have terrible handwriting.

BOB

Well, John, I noticed on your card that before you put this dog act together, you worked as a parakeet trainer . . . Is that right?

NORBIS

Yes.

BOB

Well, just what does that involve?

NORBIS

Well, it involves a parakeet . . . a cage . . . a chair and a whip . . . and a pistol . . . and a piece of newspaper.

BOB

And now you're working exclusively with these poodles?

NORBIS

Yes.

BOB

How many do you have?

NORBIS

Well, we have seven with us now. We started with four, but then we had three more join us in August.

BOB

Can you describe one or two of the tricks the dogs do?

NORBIS

Sure. One of the larger poodles holds a hoop and I jump through it.

BOB

That's something that hasn't been done before, has it?

NORBIS

I don't know . . . then he stands up on a chair, and I get a head start and as I go through the hoop, this time I do a twistabout . . . and then at the far end I do a somersault.

BOB

That's pretty fancy.

NORBIS

Yes. And if I do it right he gives me a dry Martini.

BOB

Does he know when . . .

NORBIS

When I do it right? Sure! They're smart dogs. Then at the end of the act, I lie down on the floor and . . .

BOB

Play dead.

NORBIS

Oh? You've seen the act?

BOB

No, I just guessed. Say, I know you have a performance tonight, so we'll let you go . . . while I welcome my second guest, about whom I know only two things: his name—which is Clinton Snideley—and the fact that he keeps wild boars in his apartment. There could be a story here . . . and let's see if we can get it. Clinton, you keep wild boars in your apartment?

SNIDELEY

Yes I do.

BOB

Why do you do that, Clinton?

SNIDELEY

I need them in my business.

BOB

Which is?

SNIDELEY

I'm a truffle hunter.

BOB

I know there is a connection between wild boars and truffles but I'm not clear on it.

SNIDELEY

Truffles are growths that appear on the roots of oak trees. And you need wild boars to sniff 'em out. You see, what I do . . . I take these wild boars across the street on a leash . . .

BOB

Where do you take them?

SNIDELEY

Up in the big park up here.

BOB

Up in Central Park.

SNIDELEY

Right. And they sniff around oak trees and wherever they sniff the most, I drive a stake into the ground. Then I bring them back across the street and put them in my apartment and get a shovel and I come back and I dig where I had the stake in the ground. Then I get these truffles. Sometimes I get them this big—I get three dollars for a truffle that size.

BOB

Pretty expensive, huh?

SNIDELEY

I sell them to Julia Child . . . people like that.

BOB

Do you get into any trouble with the authorities, taking your wild boars around the oak trees in the park?

SNIDELEY

No. I get a lot of crank phone calls from my neighbors in the wee hours of the morning—and a lot of unsigned mail—but that all tapers off at Christmas time when they get the smoked ham.

BOB

A little payoff you have going there. Let me ask you this . . . maybe this hasn't occurred to you but it has to me . . . Don't you think it's a little bit unfair to keep a pack of wild boars penned up in one small room of a small apartment here in the city?

SNIDELEY

What do you care how I take care of my wild boars?

BOB

Well, I'm an animal lover . . .

SNIDELEY

Wait a minute! Wait! Let me finish! What am I supposed to do with these wild boars?

BOB

I don't know.

SNIDELEY

I can't let 'em run free.

BOB

No . . .

SNIDELEY

They're wild beasts, ya know that? What would you do if you had a bunch of wild boars?

BOB

Well, I . . .

SNIDELEY

That's the trouble with you fellas . . . you put your foot in it all the time.

BOB

Well . . .

SNIDELEY

I came here to talk about wild boars, truffles, maybe a recipe or two . . .

BOB

Right.

SNIDELEY

Suddenly, you're an animal lover, and I'm some kind of a nut!

BOB

Well . . .

SNIDELEY

I don't need this! No way! I'm going home!

BOB

Well, all right . . . I'm sorry . . .

SNIDELEY

I don't even own a TV set—so I can't see your show!

BOB

Clinton Snideley, Truffle Hunter, has been our guest, ladies and gentlemen.

Galaxy of the Baboons

("Theme from 2001: A Space Odyssey." Establish and fade for)

RAY

And now we invite you to journey with us through space and time to the distant future for another strange story from . . .

BOB *(echo chamber)*

The Galaxy of the Baboons!

RAY

For our latest weird adventure, we move through a time warp to the year 6128. A superior race of monkeys has taken over the universe. And—as darkness settles over the barren landscape—we find one of the creatures loping through the entrance of his dwelling place . . .

(Door slams)

HAROLD

I'm home, Margaret. Where the devil are you?

MARGARET

Is that you, Harold?

HAROLD

Yes—yes. Of course it's me. Who were you expecting—King Kong?

MARGARET

Harold, I don't know why you have to come home in such a foul mood every night. Baboons are supposed to be cute and friendly.

HAROLD

Well, I don't know what you expect. Our pet human wasn't out at the front gate to meet me when I came home. And I see he hasn't even fetched the evening paper. Where is he? Asleep under the porch again?

MARGARET

I really don't know. He was playing with his ball in the yard just a little while ago. But don't get yourself all upset about it. I'll have dinner on the table in a few minutes.

HAROLD

I wish we didn't have to eat as soon as I get home every night, Margaret. I'd like to unwind by swinging in my tire out in the yard for a while before dinner.

MARGARET

Well, it just makes it so late when I get through in the kitchen. All this housework is driving me bananas.

HAROLD

Margaret—I wish you'd stop using that expression. It seems to reflect on our heritage somehow.

MARGARET

I'm sorry. It was only a figure of speech. My! You are in a grouchy mood tonight.

HAROLD

Well, I've had a hard day at the plant. Moberly called in sick. Colgrove's still on his vacation. And everything falls on my shoulders.

MARGARET

Was Colgrove the one I met at the company picnic last summer? A little short monkey with a speech impediment?

HAROLD

No. That's Gunderson. Colgrove's a tall gorilla.

MARGARET

I guess I don't know him then.

HAROLD

What?

MARGARET

I said I don't know him. I never met the ape.

HAROLD

Well, the way you swallow your words—I can't hear half of what you say.

MARGARET

Well, I'm sorry. I was just talking to myself anyway.

HAROLD

About what?

MARGARET

About Colgrove. I was trying to think if I knew him. But I guess I don't.

HAROLD

What?

MARGARET

I said I don't know Colgrove.

HAROLD

Well, you haven't missed much. Anyway, he's on vacation this week.

MARGARET

Yes. You mentioned that. Now do sit down at the table and eat something. I've had a dreadful day—picking fleas off the children all afternoon.

HAROLD

It's been rough at the plant, too. Having two monkeys out at once puts everything on my shoulders. But the boss doesn't care. Just so the work gets done by somebody.

MARGARET

I suppose that's true.

HAROLD

What?

MARGARET

I said I suppose it's true that nobody cares how hard you have to work.

HAROLD

That's the way it seems to me, too, Margaret. But at my age, I just have to keep scrambling to stay ahead of the young baboons who are after my job. Only today, one of them claimed I'm getting hard of hearing.

MARGARET

Well, that's a terrible thing to say to you.

HAROLD

What?

(Theme: establish and fade for)

RAY

And so we journey back across the endless reaches of space and time to our own world as we know it. But soon, we'll be making another fantastic voyage into the future—when we'll hear Harold say . . .

HAROLD

Odd. They never picked up the trash on Wednesday before.

RAY

That's in the next strange episode of . . .

BOB *(Echo chamber)*

The galaxy of the baboons.

The Overstocked Warehouse

BOB

Friends, the great Bob and Ray Giant Overstocked Surplus Warehouse —which has done it so many times before—has just succeeded in doing it again.

RAY

We know it sounds too good to be true, neighbors. But our alert staff has purchased the entire stock of the nation's largest bankrupt taxidermist for a fraction of what would have been a ridiculous price even if we had paid the whole thing.

BOB

Now we're passing the savings along to you, the consumer—and the stuffed owl of your dreams can be yours at last for an unbelievable amount plus postage and handling charges.

RAY

Which are also unbelievable.   .

BOB

Exactly. Now, friends, please don't get the idea that these are used owls or taxidermy rejects. Each and every one is freshly stuffed, bright-eyed, and solidly perched on a beautiful simulated tree branch.

RAY

We might also mention that these are not the inferior screech or hoot owls usually offered by less reliable mail order firms. Each of these handsome creatures is guaranteed for a full thirty days to be a genuine barn owl.

BOB

Now, you're probably wondering how any legitimate concern can offer purebred stuffed barn owls at a price within the reach of even the lower middle income group.

RAY

Frankly, we wondered about that ourselves until the true facts came to light. The unfortunate taxidermist whose stock we secured bought four thousand dead owls during the great bull market of 1981, only to find that they could not be stuffed and sold at a price to compete with imported Japanese owls.

BOB

Needless to say, the Japanese owls did not hold up under heavy use or severe climate. In fact, some of them proved to be nothing more than simulated feathers glued onto plastic frames. But this discovery came too late to prevent financial ruin for many domestic owl stuffers. And now, their loss can be your gain—if you act quickly.

RAY

Right. There isn't a moment to lose, friends. The Bob and Ray Giant Overstocked Surplus Warehouse still has a good selection of both male and female stuffed owls mounted on a variety of walnut, mahogany, and Early American maple twigs. But how long can a mere four thousand birds last in a nation of two hundred and forty million?

BOB

Simple arithmetic spells out the answer. More than two hundred and thirty-nine million Americans are doomed to disappointment. And you could well be one of them unless your order goes into the mail today.

RAY

As an added inducement for promptness, the warehouse is making this special bonus offer: If your order is postmarked before midnight tonight, you will receive, at no additional charge, a lovely Sanforized tee shirt bearing the cleverly worded inscription: "I shop at the Bob and Ray Giant Overstocked Surplus Warehouse in one convenient location and save money besides being open every evening until nine."

BOB

We're offering these tee shirts absolutely free of charge because we decided after they were delivered that the inscription doesn't quite make sense.

RAY

Yes. In any other form of advertising, it probably would—but on a tee shirt, not quite.

BOB

However, they do come in small, medium, and large.

RAY

But please remember, friends, it's the tee shirts that come in a choice of sizes and the stuffed owls that come in a choice of wooden twig perches. So don't forget to specify what you mean by which when you order.

BOB

But, in either event, don't delay. Even if you forget to specify what you mean by which when you order, the worst you can wind up with is a small owl and a mahogany tee shirt.

RAY

But only if it's postmarked before midnight tonight.

BOB

Right. So do it now. Just address your order to Bob and Ray—Underpriced Birds—New York.

The Hobby Hut

BOB

And now it's time to pay another of our regular visits to the Bob and Ray Hobby Hut. This is the special feature conducted by Neil Clummer, the editor of *Wasting Time Magazine*. Neil is nationally known as Mr. Hobby himself. And I see that he's getting set up over at our other microphone with his special guest for today. So we'll just let you pick it up from there and carry on, Neil.

CLUMMER

Well, thanks very much, Bob. I think the gentleman here beside me has a collection that will be the envy of every hobbyist. His name is Parnell W. Garr. Of course, that immediately rings a bell with all you listeners who collect odd-shaped fruit and vegetables. But for the benefit of the nonhobbyist, I wonder if you'd tell us something about your collection, Parnell.

GARR

Yes. I'd be happy to, Neil. My collection consists of odd-shaped fruit and vegetables. And I've traveled all over the country to assemble the prize pieces I brought with me today. I'm always reading in the paper about somebody who's grown a hubbard squash in the shape of an elephant—or something like that. So I usually hop the next plane to go dicker with the owner about buying it for my collection.

CLUMMER

And then I assume you keep the specimens in these paper sacks you brought with you today.

GARR

Yes. There aren't any ready-made albums available for displaying strange items of produce. And buying plane tickets to travel around the country picking up the stuff takes a lot of money. So I cut corners by keeping the collection in two hundred and thirty-eight separate paper sacks. I brought about twenty of the best ones with me today.

CLUMMER

Well, it's too bad that there aren't any albums available for what you collect, Parnell. But I see that you have labels neatly pasted on each sack telling what's inside and where you got it.

GARR

Yes. I try to put all that information down while I still remember the pertinent details. Like this one here. You can see that it identifies the contents of the sack as a cluster of five carrots all grown from a single seed and attached to each other at the top. I obtained those in August of 1974 from an elderly gentleman in Minnesota. And here at the bottom, it lists the price I paid—three dollars and twenty-five cents.

CLUMMER

Well, that's certainly cheap enough for an unusual specimen like five carrots all attached to each other.

GARR

Yes. The old man needed money—so he let them go cheap. But, of course, my transportation to Minneapolis from my home in Florida ran almost four hundred dollars. So I have more invested than you might think.

CLUMMER

Yes. I'm sure you do. And I notice another sack here that's labeled "Cantaloupe in the shape of a dill pickle." That's hard to imagine. I wonder if you could remove some of your prize specimens like that from their sacks so we could describe them for our listeners.

GARR

You mean you want me to open up the sacks, huh?

CLUMMER

Yes—if you don't mind. I see you just have a strip of tape across the top of each one holding it shut. So it shouldn't be too hard to put them back after we've seen them.

GARR

No. It won't be hard. So if you're sure that's what you want—okay.
(Sound: rattling of paper sack)

CLUMMER

Whew! ! ! ! That smells terrible.

GARR

Yeah. I know. That's why I couldn't figure out why you wanted me to open the sacks. Some of this fresh produce is four or five years old now. See? The date on this cantaloupe in the shape of a dill pickle is September fourteenth, 1972.

CLUMMER

Just get it away from me! I don't want to see the date. That stench is really overpowering.

GARR

Yes. That's why I keep the specimens in sacks with the tape across the top that way. There doesn't seem to be any way to preserve odd-shaped fruit and vegetables so they keep their odd shape.

CLUMMER

Well, all you've got there now is garbage.

GARR

I suppose you could say that. But of course, I can visualize what each item looked like when it was still fresh. That's why I always take a plane to go and pick up the stuff—so I can see it at least once before it decays. Like this one here—a tomato that grew in the shape of a chicken.

(Sound: rattling of paper sack)

CLUMMER

Oh, gosh ! ! ! That smells worse than the first one.

GARR

Yeah. Well, a three-year-old tomato that's not refrigerated will tend to do that.

CLUMMER

Well, would you please close the sacks up and seal them again?

GARR

I thought you said you wanted to see the stuff.

CLUMMER

No. I changed my mind. Now just get all that stuff out of here. Whew ! ! ! What a stench!

GARR

Yeah. I guess it's really not the kind of a collection I should put on display. So I'll just take it and leave. Good-bye.

CLUMMER

Well, that seems to close out another of our informative sessions here in the Hobby Hut. So until next time, this is Neil Clummer urging all of you to have a good day—and find a good hobby. (Off mike) Can we spray something in here to get rid of this?

Wally Ballou and the Common Man's Views

RAY

There's one type of reporter's assignment that's been an old standby in newspapers, radio, and television. Editors always seem to want the views of the man in the street whenever there's a controversial news development. It's hard to say why we value the wisdom of the common man so highly . . . but no matter. Here's ace Bob and Ray reporter Wally Ballou . . .

(Street background)

BALLOU

——ly Ballou seeking the views of some passersby on the latest speech from the White House. Er . . . would you step over here please, sir?

MAN

You want to talk to me?

BALLOU

Yes, sir. Did you hear the President's speech about the economy?

MAN

More or less. I was trimming the cat's toenails, but the TV was on in the other room. I could hear somebody talking and the voice sounded familiar.

BALLOU

It was the President?

MAN

Yeah. I recognized his voice from the other room.

BALLOU

Well, we're getting the reaction of people like yourself to his address. For instance, his point about declining productivity being a major cause of inflation . . .

MAN

Absolutely. You take that laundromat on the corner. Their dryers used to give you ten minutes for a dime. Now, it's up to fifteen cents but they only run for eight minutes.

BALLOU

But when the President spoke of productivity . . .

MAN

I understood him perfectly—and I agree. Take the elastic in my shorts. It never gets dry in eight minutes. So, I'm stuck for an extra fifteen cents. Right?

BALLOU

I guess so. Now, the President also talked about cutting back foreign imports.

MAN

Let me finish my thoughts on this productivity thing. See? My sister-in-law owns one of those doughnut shops where they've got a machine in the window that makes the doughnuts.

BALLOU

I'm sure your sister-in-law has her problems with the economy too, but . . .

MAN

She's got no problems. I've got problems. I work there, I sprinkle the chocolate sprinkles on the doughnuts as they go by.

BALLOU

Sir, we're talking about things like Japanese automobiles here.

MAN

What I'm telling you is that my sister-in-law speeded up the machine last week—but I still get paid the same. Now, is that justice?

BALLOU

No, I suppose not. But does that mean you agree or disagree with the President about declining productivity causing inflation?

MAN

Let me put it this way: In our parents' time . . . should a man like me —who's at the peak of his earning power—have to go around with damp elastic in his shorts?

BALLOU

Did you say you heard the speech or not?

MAN

Part of it. From the other room. My TV's in the kitchen. But I was trimming the cat's toenails. And you don't want toenails flying around the kitchen, so . . .

BALLOU

Of course not. And I appreciate getting your thoughtful insight on the President's address. Now, this is Wally Ballou . . . sending it back to our main studio.

This Place for Heroes

(Music: Documentary theme. Establish and under for)

BOB

Now . . . welcome to *This Place for Heroes*—a dramatic re-creation of events in the lives of ordinary people who have battled for the common good without giving thought to their own personal safety. Today's dramatization tells the heroic tale of up-and-coming young prizefighter, Kid Quertus. And we'll be meeting the real Kid Quertus . . . right after our factually documented story.

(Theme up and out)

QUERTUS *(fading in)*

So that's the way I feel about it, Packy. It doesn't make any difference if they don't pay me at all for fighting Killer Musgrove. I still want you to set up the match. Somebody has to take on that bully, if the noble art of boxing is to survive.

PACKY

Now, now, now, me boy. Don't go getting yourself all riled up. This Killer Musgrove is no mere bully, you know. He's a madman, he is. And they'd be barring him from the ring for life—if he wasn't heavyweight champion of the whole state of Connecticut.

QUERTUS

That's exactly why somebody's got to stop him, Packy. He kicks and gouges and half kills every opponent he meets. But they won't take his license away until there's a new state champ. And that's going to be me.

PACKY

And what, might I ask, gives you the idea you can whip Killer Musgrove? You think you're so high and mighty. Why, I've seen Killer make mincemeat out of bruisers who outweigh you by fifty pounds, me boy.

QUERTUS

Maybe so, Packy. But in my case, there's one big difference. I have decency and righteousness on my side. It's my mission to rid the fine old sport of boxing of dirty fighters like Killer Musgrove. And I'll gain strength just from knowing that honest people all over Connecticut are with me in spirit.

PACKY

I do admire your moxie, Kid. But let's not be getting carried away by the melody of our own voice. There's others charged with the job of keeping boxing clean. That's no affair of yours.

QUERTUS

Well, I'm making it my affair, Packy. The boxing commission's even more afraid of Musgrove than all the heavyweights in the state. So now, he's there on top with nobody who'll stand up to him. His dirty methods are paying off, Packy. Think of the example that's setting for all the young people in this state. Do you have any idea how many children there are in Connecticut?

PACKY

No. But there must be thousands.

QUERTUS

You bet there are. And I'm not going to let them grow up thinking that the way to succeed is to gouge and cheat and fight dirty. I'll get into the ring against Killer Musgrove and beat him fair and square—for the good of our young people—for the good of all Connecticut.

PACKY

You've already inspired me, Kid. I'm with you all the way.
                    (*Theme up full and then fade for*)

RAY

The big match was arranged—and Kid Quertus drew his strength from little people everywhere to achieve the seemingly impossible. The Kid knocked out Killer Musgrove to put the Connecticut state championship back into the hands of good, clean, decent people. The sport of boxing was saved. And it was the heroism of Kid Quertus that saved it. Now, let me ask the real Kid Quertus to come out here and receive the tribute he justly deserves.
                            (*Applause*)

QUERTUS

I'll be right there. It's a little hard to use crutches when both arms are broken, too.

RAY

I see now that you have both of them in a cast—along with one of your legs. And I really can't understand how you managed to beat Killer Musgrove on a T.K.O. after he broke that many of your bones.

QUERTUS

Oh, he didn't hurt me like this in the fight. I beat him with a lucky punch in the first round. Then Killer really got mad. Up to that point, he'd only despised me. But when I took his title away from him on a fluke, he took it personally—and worked me over out at my house the next day.

RAY

Well, I know what a painful experience that must have been. But you did win the Connecticut heavyweight championship. And nobody can take that away from you—just by throwing a temper tantrum.

QUERTUS

That's true. Nobody can take it away from me. Of course, they've taken away my car and my furniture and my house to pay medical bills. But the championship has no cash value. So they let me keep that.

RAY

Well, that mythical crown is one you can wear proudly, Kid. It's your badge of courage for all the world to see. You're a hero, Kid Quertus— the very kind of hero we're proud to honor, here on . . . *This Place for Heroes.*

(*Theme up briefly and then out*)

Einbinder Flypaper #3

BOB

Now . . . a special message for parakeet owners. Friends—do you have trouble putting insect poison in out of the way places where your bird won't eat it? If so, it's time you switched to Einbinder Flypaper for the sake of your defenseless pet. Impartial laboratory tests show that flypaper is seldom fatal to parakeets—even when they fly directly into it.

RAY

A few feathers may stick to the paper and be pulled out. But eventual full recovery has occurred in eighty-three percent of all test cases. So, for safety's sake—get Einbinder Flypaper . . . the brand you've gradually grown to trust, over the course of three generations!

The Most Beautiful Face Contest

RAY

This past weekend in Ocean City, New Jersey, they crowned the winner of the year's Most Beautiful Face Contest—and we've been granted the first interview with that winner . . . Will our lovely guest come out, please?

BODRY

I'm right here. You're looking at the winner!

RAY

Hey, wait a minute . . . you're a man, right?

BODRY

That's right.

RAY

You must be the first man to have won the Most Beautiful Face Contest.

BODRY

I believe I am.

RAY

Well . . . gee . . . I was all set to talk to a young lady . . . I don't know if my questions are particularly appropriate . . . Your vital statistics?

BODRY

Seven and a half—fifteen and a half—thirty-two.

RAY

Let's get to the fundamentals. What is your name and where are you from?

BODRY

Fahnstock P. Bodry, from Moline, Illinois.

RAY

Well, congratulations, Fahnstock. Incidentally, I have been requested by the Most Beautiful Face Committee to remind you of the obligations you assumed when you were crowned a few moments ago. You know, of course, you'll be showing your beautiful face all over this country of ours this coming year?

BODRY

Yes. Will I be chaperoned on that tour?

RAY

I'm sure you will be. Incidentally, should you do anything to bring disgrace to or cause public scorn to fall upon the Most Beautiful Face Contest, Committee, and/or its sponsors, then your title will automatically pass to the first runner-up.

BODRY

I don't plan to do anything wrong.

RAY

Well, the Committee just can't take that chance. Now, Fahnstock, can you tell us of the magic moment when you heard your name announced as winner. Did you cry a little?

BODRY

Oh, a little, I guess. I guess you could say I was dumbfounded. That's how I'd describe it.

RAY

Now that I look at you . . . you know I think you really do have a beautiful face at that.

BODRY

Yes, my cleanly chiseled features stand out.

RAY

Classic Grecian, I'd say.

BODRY

I'm told they're Roman.

RAY

I don't know. I know your eyes are well set apart. Tell me . . . how did you come by all this beauty?

BODRY

Well, both my parents were pretty.

RAY

Do you have any pretty brothers and sisters at home?

BODRY

No, I'm a beautiful only child.

RAY

Well, are you the least bit . . . er . . . self-conscious . . . I mean are you . . .

BODRY

Embarrassed to be so beautiful?

RAY

Yes.

BODRY

No, I'm used to it by now.

RAY

You get used to that. Do you find women stopping and staring at your beautiful face on the street?

BODRY

Yes, but I get used to that too.

RAY

Well, as a possessor of a beautiful face, do you take any particular precautions? Like when you shave, for instance?

BODRY

No, but I use a fresh blade every day.

RAY

Well, how about the wintertime? Do you put a protective muffler about your face to protect your features from the cold?

BODRY

No, I just walk with my back to the wind.

RAY

Well, you know, this year, like all happy times, will *fly* by for you, Fahnstock. Have you given any thought to the future? Is it Hollywood and the movies or a television career or what?

BODRY

Oh, I've thought about that life of glitter and tinsel and glamour and so forth. But I've really decided against it.

RAY

Oh?

BODRY

Yes. I don't want to be just another beautiful face!

Anxiety

RAY

And now, it's time for another story of drama and tense emotion . . . a tale well-designed to keep you in . . .
(Organ: sting)

RAY

Anxiety! . . . Here with us again to set the stage for our latest thriller is the noted author and world traveler, Commander Neville Putney. Commander, I'm sure you've reached into your amazing file and brought forth another tale well-designed to keep us all in . . . Anxiety!
(Organ: stinger)

PUTNEY

Oh, indeed I have, young man. Today's hair-raising yarn concerns two promising young bank tellers named Warren Hughie and Weldon Glimbiter. Both had received considerable praise from their branch

manager for displaying the ability to make change and add figures correctly. It seemed as if promotion for the pair were almost certain. Then, one terrible mistake brought them face-to-face with . . . Anxiety!
(Organ: stinger)

PUTNEY

The two heroes of today's drama had struck up a casual friendship with one of the bank's wealthy clients who chanced to be president of the Amalgamated Step Ladder Company. It was he who tipped them off that Amalgamated was about to unveil a new model that would glow in the dark. Warren and Weldon saw a chance to double their money overnight by embezzling funds from the bank to buy Amalgamated stock. They were certain they could replace the money before it was missed. But as Weldon returned to his desk after phoning the stock broker to sell at a big profit, his eyes were downcast. Warren noticed immediately.

WARREN

Weldon—I noticed immediately that your eyes are downcast. But you don't need to feel bad if we failed to double our money overnight. I'll gladly settle for a gain of fifty percent. Just so we can sell out and replace what we embezzled before Mr. Prouty notices the shortage.

WELDON

I wish it were possible to settle for a gain of fifty percent—or even to break even, Warren. But when I phoned our broker and told him to sell Amalgamated Step Ladder—he said he couldn't give it away at any price.

WARREN

Good gravy, Weldon. I don't understand. This is the day when the new Amalgamated glow-in-the-dark model was to be introduced. Did our broker say why that development had caused the stock to go down?

WELDON

No. He just said that Amalgamated Step Ladder had dropped as far as it could go—and that we should have known it was a risky investment when we bought it.

WARREN

Good gravy, Weldon. It's small wonder that you returned to face me with downcast eyes. We're in a real pickle.

WELDON

True. It's also a fine kettle of fish.

WARREN

Well, I think it goes without saying that this is a fine kettle of fish. But the thing that raises it to the level of a real pickle is the fact that we didn't just lose our own money, Weldon. We've embezzled funds from the bank—and we'll go to the hoosegow for sure when the shortage is discovered.

WELDON

Yes. There's no doubt about that, Warren. Buying stock in Amalgamated Step Ladder seemed like a surefire way to get rich quick. Instead, that one little mistake has wiped out two promising careers. Now, we'll be packed away in the hoosegow until we both rot.
(Organ: stinger)

RAY

Boy, oh boy, Commander. That story really had me perched on the edge of my chair. But you can't just leave us all in anxiety this way. Did Weldon and Warren throw themselves on the mercy of the court —and somehow miraculously escape a long term in prison?

PUTNEY

No. As I recall, they merely sold their Amalgamated Step Ladder stock at a profit of several hundred thousand dollars. So of course, that enabled them to replace the bank funds they'd stolen, and still have plenty left over to retire to the French Riviera.

RAY

But I don't understand, Commander. In your story, Weldon and Warren's broker told them that Amalgamated Step Ladder had dropped as far as it could go—and that he couldn't even give it away.

PUTNEY

Oh, my no, young man. That was only a momentary misunderstanding. You see, Weldon dialed a wrong number and reached some house painter by mistake instead of his stock broker. As chance would have it, the painter had just tumbled off an Amalgamated Step Ladder at work. So in a fit of pique, he naturally answered Weldon's inquiry about Amalgamated by saying that it was worthless and risky because it had just fallen as far as it could go.

RAY

Commander, that is the most ridiculous story I ever heard in my life.

PUTNEY

I quite agree. And Weldon and Warren got a hearty chuckle out of it themselves once they discovered the silly error they'd made. I'm glad to see you find it amusing too. (chuckles)

RAY

I didn't say I found it amusing, Commander. The word I used was ridiculous. And I don't think Weldon and Warren got a chuckle out of it, as you claim—because I don't think Weldon and Warren ever existed. You just made up the whole dumb thing.

PUTNEY

Why, you cheeky young blighter. You haven't the vaguest notion of what you're talking about. Now I'd suggest that you read your closing announcement before you find yourself in very serious trouble.

RAY

Well, after that clinker, I think we're both in serious trouble. But I'll try to get through this closing announcement . . . Friends, join us again next time when Commander Putney will again reach into his amazing file and bring forth a tale well-designed to keep you in . . . Anxiety!

(Organ: stinger)

Edible Food Packaging

RAY

The Patent Office has issued a patent to a manufacturer who plans to turn out food products wrapped in packages which are, in themselves, edible. We've come to this supermarket in King of Prussia, Pennsylvania, to get the reaction of a person who would be dealing first-hand with this new development in food processing, Checker-Outer Number Twenty-Three. His name is Leonard Bonfiglio. Leonard . . . have you heard of the edible food package?

BONFIGLIO

No, sir, I haven't.

RAY

Well . . . we came all the way down here to King of Prussia, Pennsylvania, to get your reaction. It's a package you can eat . . . You haven't heard about it?

BONFIGLIO

No, sir, I haven't.

RAY

Well . . . as long as we're here, let's see if we can get a human interest story . . . a supermarket human interest story . . . er . . . Leonard . . . does this Twenty-Three have any special significance?

BONFIGLIO

Yes, it means that this is checkout counter Number Twenty-Three.

RAY

You always work here on Twenty-Three?

BONFIGLIO

No. A few years ago, I used to work over on Sixteen.

RAY

Is there any difference between Twenty-Three and Sixteen . . . other than the obvious seven?

BONFIGLIO

Yes. When I worked on Sixteen, you had to take in bottle returns.

RAY

We're talking with Leonard Bonfiglio here in a supermarket in King of Prussia, Pennsylvania. We came to get his reaction to the edible food package story, but it seems that he hasn't heard about it. Now we're trying to get a human interest story. Leonard . . . what's the favorite food that you like to check out?

BONFIGLIO

I guess I like to check out sirloin steak.

RAY

Well . . . conversely, is there any food that you don't like to check out?

BONFIGLIO

I don't like to check out shepherd's pie . . . or canned Brunswick
stew . . .

RAY

I guess we could all go along with you on that. Leonard . . . what's the
biggest amount you ever rang up on one single sale?

BONFIGLIO

A hundred and ninety-three dollars and sixty-two cents.

RAY

Wow!

BONFIGLIO

It was a holiday weekend.

RAY

Fourth of July?

BONFIGLIO

I don't know. I do remember it was summer. The order included two
twenty-pound bags of charcoal.

RAY

Incidentally, if you like to cook with charcoal, be sure to use it outdoors.
Cooking with charcoal indoors, there's a danger of carbon monoxide
poisoning.

BONFIGLIO

I never heard about that.

RAY

This is Leonard Bonfiglio, here in a supermarket in King of Prussia,
Pennsylvania. We're trying to get a human interest story. Leonard?
Any important people ever come through here? Any celebrities?

BONFIGLIO

Yes. Xavier Cugat came through here once. He had his chihuahua with
him.

RAY

I didn't know they allowed dogs in supermarkets.

BONFIGLIO

They don't usually, but he had it in his pocket, and I guess they over-
looked it or something.

RAY

I'm getting a hurry-up signal here. Leonard, is there any supermarket
anecdote, any supermarket joke, you fellas like to tell each other?
Anything to lighten up this otherwise serious interview?

BONFIGLIO

Well, you might like this one. A fella came in here about a year ago
. . . and he came up to me and he said . . . "Before I go back inside,
I want to make sure that you can change an eighteen-dollar bill."

RAY

Oh, a wise guy, huh?

BONFIGLIO

I said: "Sure! How do you want it? Two nines or three sixes?"
(Bonfiglio shakes with laughter)

RAY

And there's our human interest story from King of Prussia, Pennsylvania!

Wally Ballou Reports on Cameras in the Courtroom

RAY

Each year, more state and local governments are allowing television cameras in their courtrooms. Today, correspondent Wally Ballou is visiting another community that will soon be taking that step. Come in, please, Wally Ballou.

BALLOU

——ly Ballou reporting from the chambers of County Judge Merton Claypool in Lost River, Ohio. Judge Claypool has handed down a ruling that will permit TV cameras in his courtroom beginning next week. Your Honor, what's the thinking behind that decision?

CLAYPOOL

Well, I've watched televised trials in other areas recently, and I decided that—comparatively speaking—I'd be a smash hit on the tube.

BALLOU

Well, you do cut an impressive figure, sir—but . . .

CLAYPOOL

It's a certain star quality that I have about me, Mr. Ballou . . .

BALLOU

I guess that's the term I was groping for . . .

CLAYPOOL

Perhaps I could show your viewers what I mean by that. It's such an undefinable thing.

BALLOU

A demonstration might help.

CLAYPOOL

Well, this is just a little piece of stage business I've been working on. But it shows how my magnetic personality reaches out and grabs an audience.
(Pounds gavel)

CLAYPOOL

The witness is directed to answer the question or be held in contempt!
(Puts gavel down and lowers his voice)
That's about it—basically.

BALLOU

Beautifully done, sir!

CLAYPOOL

Thank you. But do you think I should do it that way—banging the gavel before I yell? Or should I speak the line and then do the gavel bit at the end? You know, as sort of a snapper?

BALLOU

Gee, it's been so long since *Perry Mason.* I don't recall which works best. I think you can do it either way.

CLAYPOOL

Probably so . . .

BALLOU

But tell me, sir—when you first got the idea for letting TV into the courtroom.

CLAYPOOL

Oh, I guess I've had a little greasepaint in my blood ever since law school.

BALLOU

Really?

CLAYPOOL

Yes. We used to put on a show every year. I remember once we did a school pageant based on the Bill of Rights. I was the Ninth Amendment.

BALLOU

I don't believe I know that one . . .

CLAYPOOL

I'm not sure either, after all these years. But I think it deals with coveting thy neighbor's ox.

BALLOU

Is that in the Bill of Rights?

CLAYPOOL

I don't know. As I say, I've been out of law school for years. But I still have a newspaper review of that pageant. The critic wrote: "Young Merton Claypool handled his supporting role as the Ninth Amendment with aplomb."

BALLOU

With what?

CLAYPOOL

Aplomb. It describes first-rate acting. Years later, I read a review saying Marlon Brando had portrayed the Godfather with aplomb. So Brando and I have the same thing.

BALLOU

Then you really approve of having cameras in court just so you can put on a performance?

CLAYPOOL

Why not? I never say anything I wouldn't want your kids to hear.

BALLOU

But a man could be on trial for his life . . .

CLAYPOOL

Not in my court. They don't let me handle that big stuff. In fact, I'll be opening next week in the case of the Elmdale Water District versus the State Public Utilities Commission.

BALLOU

Well, it sounds as if that one will need all the punching up your talent can give it, Judge. So good luck and now, this is Wally Ballou, saying . . . until next time . . . This is Wally Ballou saying so long.

The Four-Leaf Clover Farmer

BOB

We came across a gentleman in Henderson, Vermont, recently. His name is Nelson Malamon, and his story struck us so much that we invited him to tell it himself.

MALAMON

And I want to thank you and the generous Bob and Ray organization for underwriting my trip, too. It's a wonderful experience.

BOB

You deserve it . . . particularly with the run of bad luck you've had. Tell everyone what it is you do, Nelson.

MALAMON

Well, I own a four-leaf clover farm back in Henderson. I developed a breed of hybrid four-leaf clovers some years ago.

BOB

And you found a market for them?

MALAMON

That's right. I sell them to novelty makers who put them into little plastic cases as good luck tokens . . .

BOB

I've seen those. I used to get one of those from my insurance man every year.

MALAMON

Right. Anyway, I thought this was going to be a banner year for my business until last June.

BOB

That's when your troubles started.

MALAMON

It was Friday the thirteenth—that's the funny part—and my assistant, Neil, was taking my entire first crop by truck to Bellows Falls. From there it goes to my biggest customer in New York.

BOB

What happened?

MALAMON

The truck went over a cliff and we lost the entire crop. Neil was unscathed, however.

BOB

He was lucky, anyway.

MALAMON

My second crop came out rather badly. It takes about six weeks for a crop to be ready for harvest.

BOB

I was going to ask you that.

MALAMON

I couldn't tend it properly because I was laid up . . . I got hit in the head with a horseshoe that was hanging over the door of my greenhouse.

BOB

Yes, I can still see the lump there.

MALAMON

No. That's the way it always was!

BOB

Well, go ahead.

MALAMON

Besides me being laid up, the crop-dusting plane crashed, so a lot of the clovers ended up with leaves eaten away—and there's nothing more worthless than a four-leaf clover with only two or three leaves!

BOB

I agree. Looks like this whole year past will have to be written off as a disaster.

MALAMON

You know the rest. The day you visited me back in Henderson was the day the telephone pole fell on my greenhouse—destroying the entire third crop.

BOB

And that bit of misfortune involved your neighbor, if I remember correctly.

MALAMON

Yes. He raises hares . . . for rabbits' feet. Well, he had his truck laden with rabbits' feet and was headed for Bellows Falls . . . when he swerved to avoid hitting a black cat . . .

BOB

. . . and hit the pole—knocking it onto the greenhouse.

MALAMON

Hardly any wonder you thought my story worthy of telling on Friday the thirteenth!

BOB

Right, and you certainly have had a tough time this year.

MALAMON

Well things are looking up, though. I recently met a glass blower, and we're going into business. He's made up some beautiful crystal glass four-leaf clovers that'll be surefire sellers. Would you like to see them?

BOB

Sure would.

MALAMON

I'll get them.

BOB

And so I guess you'd say there's a silver lining behind every dark cloud. Mr. Malamon's story of incredible bad luck apparently has a happy ending after all . . .

(*Loud crash of glass backstage*)

BOB

On second thought . . .

Search for Togetherness

(Dramatic organ music. Establish and under for)

RAY

And now—*Search for Togetherness*—the touching story of people just like yourself, who struggle to overcome their misery in a small Midwestern town where the steel mill has been closed permanently.

(Theme up briefly and then fade for)

RAY

As our scene opens today, Doctor Honeycutt—the recently widowered young surgeon—is paying a surprise visit to the office of Sanford Bluedorn, kindly editor of the *Roaring Falls Advocate*.

(Door shuts)

BLUEDORN

Well, Doctor Honeycutt. This is a surprise visit, I must say.

HONEYCUTT

Yes, I was afraid that was the way it might seem to you, Sanford. And heaven knows—I'd hoped I wouldn't have to come here.

BLUEDORN

Now, now. There's no need to feel that way, Doctor. The people in this town have been coming to me with their problems for forty years or more.

HONEYCUTT

I know. But I thought I was made of sterner stuff than the rest of them. However, Agatha's murder trial is scheduled to go to the jury this afternoon—as you may have heard.

BLUEDORN

Yes. I've been following the case closely. And of course, my best young reporter, Lance Wakefield, is covering the case for the *Advocate*.

HONEYCUTT

That's what I've come to talk to you about, Sanford. I wish you wouldn't put too much trust in the stories that young Lance Wakefield is writing about Agatha's trial.

BLUEDORN

Oh, come now, Honeycutt. I know what you're thinking. But . . .

HONEYCUTT

No. I don't think you do know what I'm thinking, Sanford. I happen to be young Lance Wakefield's personal physician.

BLUEDORN

That has nothing to do with this. However, I know what you're thinking.

HONEYCUTT

No. I'm reasonably certain that you don't know what I'm thinking, Sanford.

BLUEDORN

But everyone in Roaring Falls is thinking the same thing, Honeycutt.

They know that young Lance Wakefield spent four years in prison for a crime he didn't commit. And they think his bitterness about that experience makes him unfit to cover Agatha's trial for the *Advocate*.

HONEYCUTT

I've been thinking the same thing, Sanford. And that's what I came here to talk to you about.

BLUEDORN

I was sure you would—sooner or later.

HONEYCUTT

Really? And yet you said that my visit here came as a surprise. Why?

BLUEDORN

Oh, I don't know. Perhaps I couldn't think of anything more appropriate to say when I saw you standing there in the doorway. After all, this visit has come as something of a surprise.

HONEYCUTT

I guess I should have known it would. I was hoping right up until the last minute that I might be able to stay away.

BLUEDORN

Nonsense, Honeycutt. There's no need to feel that way. The people in this town have been coming to me for forty years or more.

HONEYCUTT

I know. But I'm supposed to be made of sterner stuff. I'm a doctor, you know.

BLUEDORN

Yes. I'm aware of that. In fact, I believe you're the personal physician of my top young reporter, Lance Wakefield.

HONEYCUTT

That's right. And it's Lance Wakefield that I've come here to talk to you about.

BLUEDORN

Now, Doctor—I know what you're thinking. But . . .

HONEYCUTT

No. I don't believe you do know what I'm thinking. Lance Wakefield
is covering Agatha's murder trial for the *Advocate*. And that trial is
scheduled to go to the jury this afternoon.

BLUEDORN

Really? I didn't know it was going to be so soon. Lance Wakefield
hasn't filed his story on the trial for the early edition yet.

HONEYCUTT

Sanford—I wish you wouldn't put too much trust in the stories that
young Lance Wakefield is writing about Agatha's trial. That's what
I came here to talk to you about.

BLUEDORN

What is there to talk about? Lance Wakefield is my top reporter—so
naturally, I assigned him to cover Agatha's trial. I can't see that there's
anything to discuss.

HONEYCUTT

Perhaps you're right. And I guess I'd best be going. I'm sorry to have
troubled you, Sanford.

BLUEDORN

No trouble at all, Doctor. I'm glad we had this little talk. Very glad
indeed.

(Theme. Establish and under for)

RAY

And so Doctor Honeycutt has finally revealed his true feelings about
young Lance Wakefield to kindly old Sanford Bluedorn. But has the
revelation come too late to save Agatha? Perhaps we'll learn more in
the next exciting episode. Join us then for more touching drama on . . .
Search for Togetherness.

(Theme up briefly and out)

News in Depth

(Pompous news theme up full)

BOB

And now, ladies and gentlemen, it's time for one of the most eagerly awaited features on the Bob and Ray show—one that always fills a much-needed gap: Bob and Ray's *News in Depth.*
(Theme up and out)

BOB

Our first guest on *News in Depth* today is a gentleman who heads up a little-known yet vital governmental department. He's regional Eastern Interbureau Coordinator of Administration for the New England states, Ohio, and Southern Indiana. Mr. Clyde L. "Hap" Whartney.

WHARTNEY

Thank you. Everybody in Washington watches your show.

BOB

Thank you. We're very glad to hear that.

WHARTNEY

Now, I've taken the liberty to go ahead to prepare some questions and answers here so that there will be no misunderstanding as to the function of my office and just what it is we do down there in Washington. Here's our script.
  (*Takes two sets of papers from his pocket and hands one to Bob*)

BOB

Well, I was just going to fire away questions off the cuff.

WHARTNEY

It will be easier this way. Now where it says "Bob"—that's for you, see . . . and I have the answers written down here.

BOB

All right, Hap. (*He reads*)
There seems to be some confusion in many circles as to the responsibility of the World Bank vis-à-vis as to the Federal Reserve Board and Bank. Could you clear it up for us?

WHARTNEY

I'm glad you asked me that question. The Federal Reserve Board is a semi-quasi-governmental agency that operates the Federal Reserve Bank and also proposes interest rates that member institutions should charge.
  (*Pause*)

BOB

And the World Bank?

WHARTNEY

I was getting to that. The World Bank's function is to loan money, capital, that is, to emerging nations to encourage their growth. Next question?

BOB

As I understand it, the interest rate charged by banks has a definite relationship to the prime interest rate suggested by the Federal Reserve Bank.

WHARTNEY

That's not even a question. I think I know what you're *trying* to ask, though. Member banks borrow money at little or no interest in order to have funds to lend to business and individuals at prime rates.

BOB

You certainly know your subject matter. Allow me to congratulate you. So many of my guests come here and don't seem to be familiar with their own jobs.

WHARTNEY

That is very kind of you. We at Interbureau Coordination pride ourselves on our complete dedication to the serious responsibility that is squarely placed on us. I'm sure our broad shoulders will more than bear up under the tremendous pressure.

BOB

I want to thank you, Mr. Whartney, for coming here tonight, and so brilliantly describing your office and its functions. You have spruced up an otherwise ordinary program.

WHARTNEY

You are more than kind, and I might add, very discerning.

BOB

I want you to know the welcome mat is always down for you, Mr. Whartney, and the door is always open. Good guests like you are hard to come by.

WHARTNEY

Thank you, and goodnight.

BOB

We now switch to anchorman Wally Ballou, of the Bob and Ray

election coverage team, who has just predicted defeat for candidate
Neil A. Sturbush in the race for county commissioner. What makes this
interesting is the fact that Mr. Sturbush spent more money in waging
his campaign than any office seeker ever spent before. Let's go right
now to Sturbush headquarters for what will undoubtedly be a speech
of concession . . .

(Convention background)

STURBUSH

Would you all simmer down out there please . . . Simmer down . . .
(The sound fades)

STURBUSH

I guess you all heard Mr. Ballou when I did. He's predicted my defeat;
I guess I lost. Well . . . those things will happen. I'd like to say a few
words if I may . . . I know that after my opponent has been in office
a couple of months . . . the people will come to me and say . . . I wish
now I had voted for you, Sturbush. He's a bum—you're okay. Won't
you please run again? You know what I'm going to say to them?
NUTS! You had your chance to vote for me and you didn't—NUTS!
I'm not going to run again. I've spent a fortune in television and radio.
All I have left is what I've got in my pocket. In conclusion, I'd like to
say one thing . . . You're just not going to have Neil Sturbush to kick
around any more!

(Convention sounds up again)

RAY

Now to analyze Mr. Sturbush's speech, here is the Bob and Ray *News
in Depth* specialist—David Chetley. David . . .

CHETLEY

In exactly one hundred and fifty words, Neil A. Sturbush has left little
doubt that he has lost this race . . . and further, that he does not
intend to run again. With some degree of circumlocutory skill, he has
couched the absinthian vehemence of his address in a periphrastic bit
of casuistry, which is paralogistic on the one hand, and incapacious on
the other. Indeed, his jeremiad—his threnody—call it what you will—
can only be accepted for what it is: an atrabilious amphigory. This is
David Chetley.

RAY

Thank you, David. You took the words right out of my mouth!

RAY

Now—we have been asked to make the following announcement by the Treasury Department. Citizens, our money is your money. We print it for you to use. It is for your convenience. Make more use of money. It's handy, it's dependable, it's trustworthy. Money orders, checks, bank drafts, credit cards are good in their way, but money is better. It is easy to carry, transfers quickly, and is soft to the touch. It comes in a lovely green color, which is pleasant to the eye. It has pleasing pictures on it of Alexander Hamilton, George Washington, Andrew Jackson, and the White House. The numbers are large and clearly legible. If you want money, just write and tell us how much and in what denominations. Use money every day. It's the American way!

(Patriotic music)

BOB

And now back to *News in Depth,* and another guest. The story of this man's trial has been front page news in papers across the country these past few weeks. He is the corrupt Mayor of Skunk Haven, New Jersey— Mayor Ralph Moody Thayer . . . Mayor Thayer . . .

THAYER

Thank you.

BOB

Is the jury still out, by the way?

THAYER

Yes, it is. But my attorney is negotiating with the foreman of that august group now, and we feel we have nothing to fear. We believe that you can attract more flies with honey than you can with vinegar.

BOB

Mayor Thayer, to go back over your checkered career . . . You were a petty forger, a master swindler, a convicted embezzler . . .

THAYER

And convicted of perjury several times.

BOB

How does one start on a life of corruption such as you have built for
yourself?

THAYER

Oh, I guess it started when I was a kid. I used to cheat in exams in
grade school. I used to tell malicious lies about my fellow students to
the teacher. You see, I've always believed I could build myself up by
tearing somebody else down.

BOB

Now after your formal schooling was completed, I think you developed
an interest in financial matters . . . money lending . . .

THAYER

Loan sharking.

BOB

Yes.

THAYER

I did that for several years until the criminal element in town asked
me to run for public office. I took that as a mandate.

BOB

I remember that first election. It still stands as the crookedest election
in Skunk Haven's history.

THAYER

Thank you.

BOB

And from then on, it was all downhill, really . . . Over the years you've
riddled every department of your administration with corruption. All

the way from the top to, well, right on through to the Visiting Nurse
Association. I'd like to ask you a final question, Mr. Mayor, and don't
answer right away. Give it some thought, if you will. Would you say
it's easier to be corrupt today, than it was, say, ten . . . even fifteen
years ago?

THAYER

Oh my, yes! You see, ten or fifteen years ago, it was a disgrace to be
corrupt. Now it's a very fertile field. I recommend it to anybody with
a devious mind, who is willing to put in long, long hours, without
working hard. They will find it terribly enriching. Fully rewarding.

BOB

Well, I'm sure we will all be able to draw something from your words
and I want to thank you very much for coming by. We will be anxious
to hear what the jury decides when it comes back in.

THAYER

Don't give it a thought! I'm not!

BOB

Thank you, Mayor Thayer . . . And thank you all for tuning into *News
in Depth*. Before we go, however, let me remind you that . . .

RAY

The opinions expressed by our guests are their own—and do not
necessarily represent the views of the Bob and Ray organization.

BOB

Also, they should not be construed as the opinion of this station . . . or
its subscribers . . . or members of their families.

RAY

And it must also be remembered that questions asked by the panel are
not designed to reflect any particular viewpoint.

BOB

We should mention, too, that our panel members are speaking only for
themselves—and not as representatives of their employers or members
of their families.

RAY

But in any event, this program is presented solely for the enjoyment of the viewing audience . . . and any rebroadcast or reuse without specific permission is prohibited.

BOB

Likewise, any admission charged by owners of TV sets for watching this broadcast is similarly prohibited.

RAY

The entire contents of this program remain the sole property of the Bob and Ray organization—and may not be used for any commercial purpose by the New York Jets—or the commissioner of the National Football League.

BOB

That includes reproduction in whole or in part, Ray.

RAY

Absolutely, Bob. However, it should be understood that portions of this program may have been recorded earlier for broadcast in this time period.

BOB

This is done solely for the convenience of our audience—and not for the purpose of editing or deleting controversial material.

RAY

In so doing, some passages that have been retained may be considered offensive by various ethnic groups or religious organizations.

BOB

Therefore, discretion is urged among members of such groups or organizations in listening to the material presented.

RAY

Parental guidance is also suggested. And in no case shall children under the age of sixteen be permitted to listen to this program.

BOB

This ruling applies not only to the public at large—but also to employees of this station and members of their families.

RAY

Any application for exemption from this order must be received in our office before midnight tonight.

BOB

On all such applications, the decision of the judges is final . . . and in case of duplication, ties will be awarded.

RAY

However, the awarding of all prizes is subject to availability. Substitutions for announced prizes may be made at the discretion of the Bob and Ray organization.

BOB

But in any case, at least half of this program must be completed in order for it to qualify as an official broadcast.

RAY

If less than half is completed for any reason, then the entire program will be rebroadcast from the beginning at a later date—as determined by the commissioner.

BOB

That's correct. Now, was there anything else we wanted to add?

RAY

Yes, some of our departing guests will receive gift packages of our subscribers' products.

BOB

I know they'll enjoy that. Well, that brings us to the end of another broadcast day. Join us soon for another look at more controversial issues on *News in Depth.*

RAY

Research director for *News in Depth*: Carl J. "Fat" Chanz.

BOB

Our program director was O. Leo Leahy.

RAY

Producer: T. Wilson Messy. This was a Messy Production.

Now, this is Ray Goulding, saying—*wait a minute, folks*—we have an important announcement! Don't we, Bob?

Monongahela Metal Foundry #4

BOB

Yes, indeed, Ray. Here's the news you've all been waiting for from the Monongahela Metal Foundry. We've got a winner in our giant sweepstakes contest to select a trade name for Monongahela's new Number Four size steel ingot!

(Fanfare)

RAY

Our lucky first prize contestant is: Mr. Elroy K. Depew . . . of Rural Route Number One . . . in Carthage, Missouri.

(Applause)

BOB

Congratulations, Mr. Depew!

RAY

And the winning name suggested by Mr. Depew was . . . ALFRED!

(Applause)

RAY

Congratulations again to you, sir . . . and your fortune in prizes will be on its way to you first thing tomorrow. And *now* this is Ray Goulding, saying . . . Write if you get work.

BOB

And Bob Elliott, reminding you to hang by your thumbs. Goodnight, folks.

RAY

Goodnight.

"Like many inspired inventions, the creation of this magic company was accidental," wrote *The New Yorker* in 1973. "The time was 1946 and the place the Boston radio station WHDH. Bob had a morning record show and Ray gave the hourly news reports. In the manner of Sissle and Blake, Gilbert and Sullivan, Laurel and Hardy, and Ellington and Strayhorn, they discovered almost immediately that they had a telepathic bond." Proceeding to NBC, New York, in 1951, they quickly convulsed the rest of the country as well, and they have been present on the airwaves, in one form or another, ever since. Their most recent program, "The Bob and Ray Show," was heard over National Public Radio stations in the fall of 1982, and will resume in 1983. The series earned them their third Peabody Award.

Bob and Ray's achievements also include a hit Broadway show, *Bob and Ray: The Two and Only*, dubbed "one of the zaniest shows to hit town in many a season" by *The New York Times*; many award-winning commercials, including those starring the famous Piel brothers, Bert and Harry; the movies *Cold Turkey* (in which they played, successively,

Walter Cronkite, David Brinkley, and Arthur Godfrey), and *Author! Author!*; a regular segment on Hodding Carter's PBS series, *Inside Story*; and specials and appearances on every major television network and on cable. In 1981 Bob and Ray were inducted into the National Broadcasters Hall of Fame and that same year were named "Men of the Year" by the Broadcast Pioneers. In 1982, the Museum of Broadcasting in New York held a retrospective of their work, which was held over for four months and broke all attendance records.

Bob Elliott lives in New York City. Ray Goulding lives on Long Island.